Miss Fortune's
LAST MISSION

UNCOVERING A STORY OF SACRIFICE AND SURVIVAL

bright sky press
HOUSTON, TEXAS

2365 Rice Blvd., Suite 202
Houston, Texas 77005

ISBN: 978-1-931721-11-0

10   9   8   7   6   5   4   3   2   1

Library of Congress Cataloging-in-Publication Data on file with publisher.

Editorial Direction: Lucy Herring Chambers
Managing Editor: Lauren Adams
Designer: Marla Y. Garcia

Printed in Canada through Friesens

*"Dearest Mother: I've been wanting to write this letter
for some time, and now seems the time to do it.
After a lay off of a month we are back to flying missions again.
From the looks of things we will all be pretty lucky
if we get through all our missions…If I should get mine
while I am up there in the clouds,
I want you to know that I'm not afraid of going."*

– LETTER FROM CHARLES SPICKARD WRITTEN FEBRUARY 9, 1944

*"On 22nd of February 1944, an American bomber
was shot down and fell to the garden of Jan Bocek on hill Dubec
(forest Chejlava). There were crowds of people
from the surroundings gathered around the place of disaster…
Torn bodies of the crew were gathered and by German order,
the town of Pradlo bought a coffin and the remains
of the bodies were buried in the presence of the mayor Vaclav
Brezak, gravedigger Frantisek Holy and police.
There appeared a wreath on the grave after some days."*

– CHRONICLE OF PRADLO

Miss Fortune's LAST MISSION

UNCOVERING A STORY OF SACRIFICE AND SURVIVAL

WILLIAM J. BOYCE | JOHN H. TORRISON
WITH JOHN DeMERS

bright sky press

HOUSTON, TEXAS

TABLE OF
CONTENTS

FATHER AND SON IN JUNE 1984.

PROLOGUE

The call to Ray Noury was more impulse than choice.

Sitting at the computer one Sunday afternoon, I looked at the search results on my screen: an address and telephone number for "Raymond Noury" in Rhode Island. This surely wasn't the same Ray Noury who flew bombing missions with my father, William D. Boyce, in 1943. Maybe it was his son, or grandson. And even if this was the same Ray Noury, he would be nearly ninety. Would he be willing talk? Able to remember? Prepared to tell me all that my father had not?

Dad and I shared daily life until I left for college at eighteen to study journalism. I wanted to be a reporter at a big daily newspaper, searching out Stories That Matter and collecting ego-boosting by-lines. I did that for a short time and then moved on to law school. My focus shifted from the newsroom to the courtroom, where it stayed for the next twenty-five years.

When my father died in 1988, I mourned his death—along with the selective silence that defined our relationship by things left unsaid. I regretted the unasked questions, but we had a tacit under-standing: I failed to ask as much as he failed to tell.

RAY NOURY SALUTES DURING CEREMONY AT DUBEC HILL CRASH SITE IN 2009.

I learned early on that "something bad" had happened to my father a long time ago. My mother, Peggy Boyce, revealed only the most basic facts when I was older. Dad fought in World War II. He flew on a plane. He was shot in the leg. He nearly died. The doctors fixed his leg. Mom and Dad met while he was in the hospital. They fell in love, got married. I was born sixteen years later. He didn't like to talk about the war. According to my mother, that was all I really needed to know.

For a long time, that was enough. I let that be enough. My attention turned to school, to getting married, to starting a career, to raising kids. I've missed my father since 1988. Only recently have I realized that this one-time reporter also missed the biggest story of his life. That story—my father's story—was right in front of me all along. I chose not to notice it.

The desire to know more about my father's war grew slowly but steadily after he died. At first I thought it was a symptom of unfinished business. But that's not quite right. It's really unstarted business—the business of finding out what really happened and trying to understand a man whose battles continued long after the shooting stopped.

That business began in earnest with my impulsive call to Ray Noury in March 2013. I discovered he was the right person to have called. At eighty-nine years old, he was very much alive with a clear head and strong memories. He was eager to talk to the son of a waist gunner who, nearly seventy years earlier, fought next to him on a B-24 Liberator while flak and fighters rushed up to rip their plane apart.

I told Ray I wanted to know what happened to my father and the crew. He answered all of my questions, and then some. Ray's answers that day would lead me across the United States, to the Czech Republic, through stacks of decades-old letters, and back to the confusion I felt as a child trying to understand why my father still was so wounded so many years after "the doctors fixed his leg."

Ray's revelations introduced me to many other people, including an entire Czech village. The villagers speak in a language I don't understand about a time that only a dwindling number of Americans are old enough to remember. The villagers remember a B-24 crew that saved my father's life in December 1943 when "something bad" happened to him in the frozen air nearly twenty-five thousand feet above Germany.

All but one of those brothers-in-combat lost their lives a short time later, in February 1944, tumbling out of the sky onto a remote Czech hillside. By then, my father no longer flew with them. But the shock and loss of their sacrifice would ripple through his life, and the lives of many others, for decades. The ripples are still visible if you know where to look—altered lives set on unexpected paths, along with memories whose value and weight have increased with each passing year.

I did not know exactly what I was looking for when I dialed Ray's number. I knew only that it was time to begin asking the unasked questions.

BILL BOYCE AT CRILE GENERAL HOSPITAL NEAR CLEVELAND, OHIO IN 1944.

CHAPTER ONE

THE HILL

The cold slapped at my face, burning the corners of my eyes until tears started to form, as the vintage Jeep climbed through forest and village upward from the town of Nepomuk to the place on the hillside where plane met earth.

"It is good," the Czech officer said from the seat behind me, leaning forward to be heard above the shifting of gears. His English was accented but good. "It is good that you said all their names out loud."

I nodded, for I'd given my brief remarks considerable thought: all through the weeks leading up to this unexpected journey in February 2014, all through the flight to Prague, all through the eighty-kilometer drive from Prague to Nepomuk in the Czech countryside, indeed all through the ceremony that had started this day of remembrance. I had spoken each of their names aloud, the ten who perished on this hillside—I had no idea in what degree of agony—along with the one who'd survived against all odds, whom I'd traveled to meet only months earlier, before he too passed from this life.

"Ray spoke fondly of his fellow crew members when I visited him," I told the citizens of Nepomuk, honoring the survivor who had visited the town twice as an old man to receive its gratitude. "Ray also spoke with great affection of the Czech citizens who helped him after he survived a fall from the burning airplane with a damaged parachute." And there was, in that moment, someone else who needed mentioning. In my life, there was always that someone else. "If they were standing here today, I think Ray and my father would be very pleased."

Because of the midlife journey I began in early 2013, it pleased me to think of my father being pleased. As long as I'd known him, until his death from lung cancer in 1988, pleased was a condition my father struggled to achieve. It was years before I understood that his volatility wasn't my fault, and it wasn't my mother's fault either—though she handled the challenges as only a strong woman, a nurse by profession, could handle them. No, the only father I would ever know became a husband and parent only after surviving the deadly skies over Europe, where cities with names like Augsburg and Regensburg were the stuff of pre-dawn briefing nightmares.

Long before he became a buttoned-down budget manager who kept his tie knotted and his temper controlled during business hours, my father was manning his .50-caliber waist gun as the Luftwaffe took aim at his bomber. The men who died on this hillside had been with my father when all of their lives were on the line. I had traveled all this way—leaving behind the courtroom and my home and my wife and my daughters—to search for clues about my father's life in a place he never saw.

Seventy years after the B-24 Liberator bomber nicknamed Miss Fortune disintegrated under fighter attack and plummeted to the ground, I had finally come here to say the names of my father's crewmates. Combat ended for my father in December 1943 when he was wounded while shooting down an attacking Luftwaffe ME 110 from his waist gunner position, high above a factory in Augsburg, Germany. The crew members who were still able to fight kept flying for another two months until their last mission—a deadly raid on an aircraft factory in Regensburg. That mission ended about one hundred and fifty kilometers from Regensburg in a crash near Nepomuk, where they died on February 22, 1944.

The Regensburg mission was part of a military air strategy known as Big Week. Between February 20 and 25, 1944, Eighth Air Force bombers based in England and Fifteenth Air Force bombers based in Italy flew more than 3,500 daylight sorties targeting German aircraft production facilities. The Royal Air Force Bomber Command flew thousands of additional sorties at night. Some ten thousand tons of bombs rained down on German factories over the course of six days. The goal was big—to eliminate the Luftwaffe as a threat to invading Allied forces scheduled to hit the Normandy beaches on D-Day. So was the cost. The Eighth Air Force lost 137 bombers during Big Week; the Fifteenth lost eighty-nine; and the RAF lost 157. Bomber gunners and Allied fighters claimed to have downed more than five hundred Luftwaffe planes. When the week's last sortie was completed, damage to German aircraft production and heavy losses among Luftwaffe pilots had shifted the balance of air superiority over Europe in the Allies' favor.

Miss Fortune and her crew became part of the Big Week casualty count. George Goddard had been the pilot. Rexford Rhodes, Haig Kandarian, Joseph Altemus, Charles Spickard, Oscar Houser, Wayne Nelson, Harold Carter, Roy Hughes and John Goldbach were the brave men who died in that final mission. Ray Noury, the only survivior, had miraculously fallen fifteen thousand feet with a damaged parachute and landed alive in a deep drift of snow.

Before I go further, let me fill in what I did know about my family before deciding to dig deeper. My grandfather, Malton Wilfrid Boyce, came to the United States from England, a trained and admired master of sacred music for both organ and choir. His life was music: performing it as the organist and choir director at the Cathedral of St. Matthew the Apostle for thirty-six years and teaching it at Catholic University in Washington, D.C. One of his university credits came from Germany, from the University of Regensburg, the very city Miss Fortune was bombing the day it was shot down.

In his adopted country, my grandfather met and married Mary Greenwald, a widow with four children. Throughout the 1920s, the couple lived in the nation's capital and brought four children into this world: Mary, my father (Wilfred D. Boyce, though some records refer to him as "William" years before he would take that as his legal name), Edward and William. The youngest child, William, was born with a heart defect and died before reaching his teens. I often wonder how my father felt about this, so often going by his dead brother's name, making it his own legally in 1948 and giving it to me, his only child.

What I gathered about my grandfather is that he was mostly absent, particularly as far as my father was concerned. By all accounts, my grandfather's intense focus on sacred music left little time for parenting. Even when my grandfather was at home, in the family's house in the northwest corner of the District, he and my grandmother were usually busy tending to William. After the boy's death, my grandparents divorced; the relationship between Malton Boyce and my father drifted off into an estrangement that was not repaired before Malton's death in 1957. I recall the story my mother told of waiting in line at the bank with my father shortly after the war. My father pointed to another customer waiting in line and asked her, "Do you see that guy over there?" He continued, "That's my old man." They did not acknowledge each other.

My father went to school with some commitment, but bonded more profoundly with a group of boys from the neighborhood. Photos from this time show a tough-looking group. Like most parents of that age, mine worked day and night so I wouldn't have to fight my way out the way they did, so I wouldn't have to struggle against the limits that had overwhelmed them. I look at the guys my father hung out with and I see the beginnings of the man who would go to war, who would shoot down a Luftwaffe fighter trying to kill him, who would spend nearly two years in the hospital reclaiming the use of his leg.

The name "Os" turns up in some of my father's earliest letters to my mother, elusive clues to a childhood largely spent fending for himself. Os was short for Oscar, a tradesman who lived near my father's home. Surely as part of his parents' floundering marriage, my father ended up living with Os and several other "lost boys" from the neighborhood in a kind of unofficial foster home. No doubt this experience made him tougher still. Surrounded by other tough young men, forced to fend for each other in matters of life and death, my father may have experienced his first boot camp in Oscar's house.

My father left high school in January 1942 and enlisted in the Army. Though he earned a high school certificate after the war, nothing indicates he seriously considered going to college before the war or immediately afterwards—when so many veterans embraced educations paid for under the GI Bill. By the time he attended night classes at Northwestern University in the 1960s, after I was born, the burdens of a full-time job, a succession of back and stomach ailments, a heart attack and parenthood combined to put a college degree beyond his reach for good.

After the war, after nearly two years in the hospital, Dad was ready to start his life. Before that, as he was leaving the grind of high school, all he really wanted to do was get into the fight. He decided to enlist in the Army Air Corps—a combat arm of the Army that would become its own service branch, the Air Force, after World War II. Between his enlistment on July 29, 1942, and his honorable discharge on September 28, 1945, my father would get his wish.

Many children of World War II veterans remark that their fathers seldom spoke about their horrific experiences in combat. This was certainly the case with my father. The few war details deemed suitable for a young boy's ears came mostly from my mother.

In the late summer of 1944, my father was in the hospital in Cleveland, Ohio when eighteen-year-old Margaret Ann "Peggy" Lesko decided to pay him a visit before she began nursing school. They had corresponded earlier in 1944 before meeting face-to-face, inspired by my mother's inquiries to learn whether the wounded waist gunner had any information about his fellow crew member Harold Carter. I gather from clues sprinkled in letters that she had been dating Harold before he shipped out—a circumstance that, perhaps understandably, did not receive in-depth treatment in the retelling to me. Over time, the letters, photos and handwritten notes reveal my mother's initial inquiries about Harold took a back seat to her budding love for Bill Boyce.

BILL BOYCE RECEIVES A KISS FROM AN UNIDENTIFIED CELEBRITY OF THE ERA DURING A MORALE-BOOSTING HOSPITAL VISIT TO WOUNDED VETS IN 1944.

In a letter written from his hospital bed on July 29, 1944, to "Dear Peggy," my father bends over backward asking her to visit him without seeming to ask her to visit him. The result is touching and, all these years of cultural change later, more than a little endearing. "To be perfectly frank with you," he writes, "I would very much enjoy your visit—if you don't go to any unnecessary trouble—if you have already made your plans and the visit is included in them, then about all I can say is—ok! I hope that covers it—it's just a plain answer—yes!" By the next letter I have, from August 11, my Dad has barely gotten past "It was swell to hear from you again" before his circular, reluctant encouragements start up again. "I can't imagine you getting the idea that I was thinking you wouldn't come at all—I realize you are having difficulties—so what ever is most convenient to you, why that is what I want you to do." Reading these letters, I feel lucky my parents managed to get together at all.

Still, I am reassured by the notes my mother penned later beside photos pasted into an album covering August through Christmas 1944. One picture that shows my Dad with one of his wounded hospital buddies, their wheelchairs side by side, carries the hand-printed inscription: "August 25, 1944. The day we met. I went to visit him at Crile Gen. Hospital in Cleveland. The song 'Always' was popular then. I knew I liked him the first day I saw him." Not far away, on the same page, is an inscription from Christmas, describing a subsequent hospital visit. "How I enjoyed those days because I was with him. I knew I was growing very fond of him and it just couldn't end here." Best of all, my mother wrote of my father, so wounded, simply and directly as "My Bill."

Our procession ground its way up onto the hillside, passing through the village of Pradlo and back into the wintry trees. The driver kept down-shifting as the road gave way to something more like a trail, and then that gave way to something more like a path. So much of what I'd sensed briefly in the grand old city of Prague, even in the town of Nepomuk, dissipated as the trees and fields extended before us. Thinking of ten American airmen perishing on this cold hillside so very far from home made the old tragedy seem very immediate.

Stepping out of the passenger side onto wet, fallen leaves, I found my way to the memorial. The people of Nepomuk erected it there in the forest to remember the airmen who gave their lives in the struggle that set them free. These people suffered through years of Nazi occupation, indeed years of Nazi atrocities, before the end of the war—which ushered them into decades of Soviet domination. Only after the Iron Curtain fell did these men and women feel free enough to erect these monuments. When they had their freedom at last, they chose to honor the ten who died here.

The monument is somber, minimalist: ten gray cubes in a row, stretching across the ground. One for each crew member. Beyond the cubes, my eyes picked out a tall, silver obelisk standing at an angle. Though all excavated pieces of Miss Fortune were transferred to a new museum—engine parts, propellers, .50 caliber guns, hats, gloves, dog tags—the obelisk looks like another piece of the plane, impaled into the earth's heart by impact and somehow passed over in the villagers' tireless efforts at collecting, identifying and memorializing. Then, at a distance, I spotted a large plaque honoring the crew, and my steps quickened. Coming closer, I recognized the enlarged photo, taken only days before Miss Fortune's last mission. But the photo I had looked at dozens of times before struck me as somehow odd.

I realized the difference: superimposed to the right of the crew I saw one additional face. Another uniformed airman. Smiling and young. I didn't know how and I didn't know why. But the airman on the plaque in the middle of this Czech forest was my father. Although I had spent the past year searching for clues about my father and these airmen, I had not expected to encounter him here.

Time healed some of the wounds my father sustained over Augsburg when a shell exploded next to his right leg and shattered his shin.. The bone fragments eventually knitted together after dozens of surgeries, though I would always notice the missing divot in his calf muscle and the deep gouge on the front of his leg. The scar looked like the rut left by a car driving on a muddy road. Months in a hip-to-ankle cast left him with limited range of motion. For years after the war, bits of shrapnel migrated to the surface of his leg, like deadly seeds seeking the sun, and my mother would pick them out with tweezers. I suspect my parents both knew that her nursing skills would be needed at home as much as they were needed at the hospital.

If my father was not healthy at the time of his simultaneous discharge from the hospital and the Army in September 1945, he was at least reassembled. Bone chips harvested from his pelvis replaced the missing pieces of his shin and spared him an amputee's challenges. He limped out of Crile General Hospital with a pair of functioning legs, the right shorter than the left. He carried a Purple Heart and an Air Medal, both with Oak Leaf Clusters; he also brought home a set of stress-induced stomach ulcers that would plague him for the next four decades. He returned to Washington D.C. and eventually

WEDDING PORTRAIT OF BILL BOYCE AND MARGARET "PEGGY" LESKO, DECEMBER 1947.

landed a job with United Airlines in 1946; he worked at United for the next forty-plus years. Dad continued corresponding with my mother until she completed nursing school in Pittsburgh the following year and joined him in the nation's capital. They married on December 27, 1947—a date chosen to save money on flowers by taking advantage of the church's Christmas decorations.

By all kitchen-table accounts, my parents wanted to have kids right after marrying, thus joining in the procreative cascade that came to be known as the Baby Boom. Life didn't get behind their plan, and eventually the couple gave up hope of having a child. The energy they could not devote to child-rearing was directed instead towards working long hours—my father in an operations job for United, my mother as a nurse. Shift by shift and paycheck by paycheck, they pursued the economic security that had been denied them as Depression-era children and journeyed to the middle class by way of job transfers to United's offices in Denver and then Chicago. To their great surprise, my parents learned that my mother was pregnant not long after their arrival in Illinois. In 1963, sixteen years after she and my father said their vows, she gave birth to me.

Around that kitchen table in our suburb of Chicago, the combat that had left my father with his scars seemed somehow unreal. I wondered about what had happened, of course. But I knew better than to ask my father. From my mother I learned only that he had been hurt in the war, that "something bad" had happened. And I sensed, more than she ever told me, that the "something" made him the man I knew.

He was, in a word, unpredictable.

We had father-son moments worthy of a Norman Rockwell painting: mowing the grass together; sanding and painting a Pinewood Derby racer fast enough to win third place; laughing at Three Stooges films on television; riding in the car and chatting easily about baseball, one of his true loves.

But then there were moments when the words stopped. I watched as he sat silently working a crossword puzzle in a rocker, silhouetted by light from the screen door leading to the patio, smoke slowly curling upward from the ever-present cigarette. There was no telling how long the silence might last: a couple of hours, an afternoon, or for days.

At other times the clouds rolled in and the thunder echoed. He raised his voice, but never his hand. To his credit—whether from his basic character, his upbringing or his life with Oscar in that unofficial foster home—a fist never formed. But his voice was effective even as a solo instrument. The storms sometimes arrived with little warning. Eventually, during my high school years, I learned how to read his moods; lie low when he was starting to get angry; and avoid pushing the buttons that would cause him to detonate.

Then there were moments when the ulcers fired up and he got sick. His stomach would rebel, nausea and vomiting would set in, and after dragging himself home from work he would take to the couch.

When tension in the house or car began elevating, my mother would respond. Sometimes she stood toe-to-toe with him, matched him decibel-for-decibel, and told him he was out of line. Other times, she communicated a different response—out loud or silently with her eyes. *It will blow over,* she assured me. And it always did.

My mother tried to convey that my father's anger was not my fault, though in some of my clearest memories it was. Part of our self-absorption in childhood is the certainty than anything wrong in the universe has to be because of us. When we learn that it isn't, we make strides toward understanding more facets of our parents' lives and possibly our own. On the way to that destination, I nonetheless managed to provoke him from time to time.

When I was about ten, my father caught me playing with matches in the basement. Books of matches were abundant because my parents both smoked constantly; there were matches in a box next to cartons of Kents in the pantry and scattered on every flat furniture surface in the house. Playing with matches was bad enough; I then made it worse. My father walked into the basement filled with acrid smoke and asked me if I was playing with matches. I told him no. After his initial blowup, he didn't speak to me for days. I wondered whether he was going to kick me out of the house. His anger had little to do with phosphorous or flame, and everything to do with lying.

A couple of years later, my parents and I flew to Washington D.C. to visit his family. He rented a car at what was then called National Airport to take us to Virginia, but before we'd gotten very far we were clearly lost. My father's anger, his frustration, grew by the minute in ways I would understand years later. Being the one in charge, the one responsible, the one expected to know things— and failing. But I missed the cues. Sitting in the backseat, I decided to make what I thought was a good joke. "Gee," I said to the back of my father's head, "it's too bad they don't give you a rent-a-driver too." Boom. After the explosion, he turned the car around, drove back to the airport and stepped out onto the curb. Feeling no need to explain himself, he left the car running, grabbed his suitcase, walked into the terminal and caught the first flight back to O'Hare. My mother told me not to worry about it and drove us to Virginia. We had a nice visit for a few days and flew home. Dad picked us up at the airport. No mention of the rent-a-driver. It was as if his solo return trip had never happened.

One other memory stands out, set again in Virginia with my cousins over the July 4th weekend in 1976. As far as I can recall, this was the first trip I ever took by myself. I was thirteen. I tumbled off a tractor and badly broke my left elbow and arm. Even today, my arm still doesn't straighten all the way. The relatives took me to a hospital to get it set and, by and by, my father flew into D.C. to take me home. To my surprise, then and maybe now, he didn't yell at me. He was full of calm reassurance as he walked into my hospital room to gather up my belongings for the trip back.

The seriousness of the break meant that I had to wear the cast for two or three months. Then, on the very day the doctor removed it, I went out to ride my bike around our neighborhood and fell. On that same arm.

It was a bloody mess, as my father saw immediately when he got home from work, hours before my mother would get home from her shift at the hospital. Using a cloth and stinging disinfectant, he cleaned out all my wounds. As I grimaced from the sting, he could have told me a thousand stories from his two years of hospitalization during and after the war, of his many surgeries. Yet all he talked about was the Civil War, when the two armies had nothing to help with pain, only a bullet for the wounded to bite on as the doctors operated and amputated. "Sometimes," my father told me, "you just have to bite the bullet." He drove me to the hospital for an x-ray, where my injury proved to be nothing more than a scrape. And since we were at the hospital where my Mom was working that evening, we went upstairs to tell her.

That's when he exploded. All of the anger he felt toward everyone and everything, that he should have felt toward me for being clumsy and careless, he flung at my mother. It did not phase her. He was just—she would explain later—letting off steam. My father had a lot of steam.

As I grew toward adulthood, I gradually began to realize that there was not necessarily a connection between my father's outbursts and anything my mother or I did. Sometimes he was simply angry. I didn't have to understand. I just had to read the signs. I got pretty good at it.

Later, as the years passed, my father grew calmer. Perhaps he was tired, especially after a heart attack ended his rotating shifts at United and he took a less physically taxing, nine-to-five job at the airline overseeing budgets and other administrative tasks. Or perhaps he was simply farther removed from the war that, though it remained unacknowledged within our family, seemed to fuel his anger and compel his tough-guy silence. He felt he had to bite the bullet, just as those Civil War soldiers had, except that his ordeal lasted into the final years of his life.

Only on a handful of occasions did the subject of World War II arise. One time, as we were watching an episode of the TV show *M*A*S*H*, set in a mobile Army hospital during the Korean War, my father told me he'd been treated in a unit like that one; his surgeon had worn "purple pajamas." He described receiving painful daily penicillin shots, thick as honey, to combat a smoldering bone infection accompanying the shrapnel embedded in his shin. The frequent injections through a large-bore needle often meant that he could barely raise his aching arms. Another time, as we watched the multi-part documentary *The World at War*, the narrator talked about American GIs in Italy. I insensitively joked that he must have eaten some great pizzas over there. All he said, his voice flat, was, "We weren't over there eating pizzas."

By the time my father was diagnosed with terminal lung cancer in early 1988 and told he had months to live, I had become what my parents had encouraged me to be. I had earned a bachelor's degree in journalism, though instead of settling in for the duration at a daily newspaper I had gone to law school. My father lived long enough to see me graduate with a law degree in May 1988, and both parents got to meet Maria—the fellow law student who became a litigator, my wife and the mother of their two grand-daughters. My parents spoke often of the limits they had encountered, limits pressed down on them by the Depression and the war, and by the unfinished education that kept my father in the same job for the last twenty years of his career at United. They wanted me to educate myself beyond all such limits, and like a good son, I had. To my regret, I was not with my father when he died at home in Chicago in November 1988. I learned of his death in a phone call from my mother while I was working out of state.

Several weeks before he died, I gathered my courage and wrote my father a letter. I found it among the family mementos I gathered from my mother's house after her death in 1996, placed it in a storage unit, and eventually moved it into my home in Houston. This letter contained the most personal words I've ever set to paper. Although I didn't want to acknowledge this fact at the time, it was a goodbye letter.

I expressed my gratitude for the tangible gifts he and Mom had given me, starting with the first-class education already pushing me forward. I thanked him for intangible gifts: a love of words and precise expression, a keen eye for irony, an intolerance for con artists who choose a "fast tongue" over hard work. These were things my father valued in this world, and for all his anger and pain, he taught me to value them too. "I've never worked hard and done well because I wanted to please you," I wrote, knowing these words might be my last chance to reach him. "I've done well and succeeded because I am you." He did not write a letter back. I had not expected one.

I like to think that we parted on good terms during my last visit with him at home. There was no estrangement and no anger—only love, sadness and resignation as the death he had narrowly escaped over Augsburg caught up with him in a temporary hospital bed parked in the den amid get well cards, a small forest of pill bottles and an oxygen tank. But the silence was still present, too. To this day, I am glad I said to him in writing some of the things I could not say to him in person. To this day, I regret that our tacit agreement remained intact to the end of his life. We never talked about how the war affected him. And then the clock ran out.

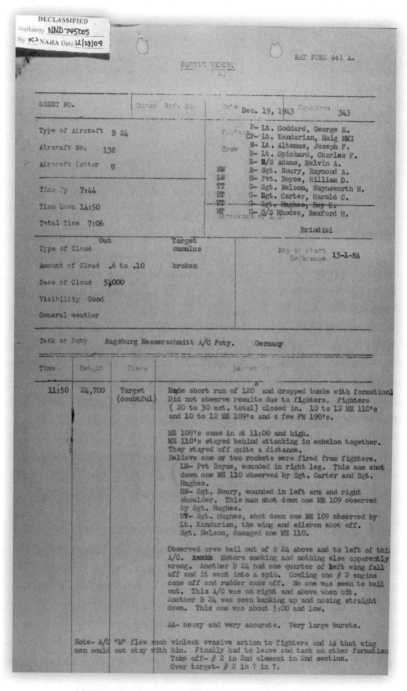

**SORTIE REPORT FOR MISS FORTUNE'S MISSION TO AUGSBURG,
GERMANY ON DECEMBER 19, 1943.**

Twenty-five years later, I discovered that I had missed a step in my life's journey. Something was missing, as surely as a hand or a foot might be missing. By 2013, that something sent me scrambling to find long out-of-print books about World War II, and to the Internet. On a website created by the granddaughter of a 98th Bomb Group pilot to turn once-classified government records into public ones, I found my first clue to what it was. This clue was a digital photograph of a declassified Air Corps sortie report.

The yellowed report was dated December 19, 1943. The bomber, part of the Fifteenth Air Force, 98th Bomb Group, 343rd Squadron, took off at 7:44 a.m. from Brindisi on the boot heel of Italy, bound for the Messerschmitt aircraft factory in Augsburg, Germany. Their bomber was a B-24 Liberator, numbered 138-U.

This aircraft reached the target at 11:50 a.m. and dropped its bombs from 24,700 feet but the crew "[d]id not observe results" because "[f]ighters (20 to 30 est. total) closed in. 10 to 12 ME 110's and 10 to 12 ME 109's and a few FW 190's." The anti-aircraft fire was "heavy and very accurate. Very large bursts." Liberator 138-U landed in Brindisi again at 2:50 p.m. In the clipped language favored by military men throughout time, here was the moment in history that propelled my father the warrior toward my mother the nurse, and that after sixteen years of marriage created me.

"Pvt. Boyce, wounded in right leg. This man shot down one ME 110." And there I read those other names, too. I would come to know them well by the time I spoke in the crisp February air in the Czech town of Nepomuk: Goddard, Kandarian, Altemus, Spickard, Adams, Nelson, Carter, Hughes, Houser and Rhodes. One name, though, grabbed my attention more than the rest—maybe because I'd seen or met him in a dimly remembered childhood experience, or had overheard my parents mention his name.

Ray Noury.

That same day, I was on the Internet searching. That same day I was on the phone to Rhode Island. That same day I was struggling through my excitement to explain to Ray who I was and why I was calling.

"I know exactly who you are," he interrupted. "I was with your father."

BILL BOYCE AND RAY NOURY AT RAY'S HOME IN RHODE ISLAND IN JULY 2013,
FIVE MONTHS BEFORE RAY'S DEATH.

CHAPTER TWO

RAY

I wrote down a neat sequence of terse factual notes during that first phone conversation with Ray Noury. These included "grabbed WDB by his harness" and "flak hit under his feet." After speaking with Ray in March 2013, traveling to Rhode Island in July 2013 to meet him in person and conducting further research following Ray's death, I would learn so many more things about my father's war and Miss Fortune's final mission; these things now seem so elementary. Those initial notes provide a stark reminder that after twenty-five years of living with my father and twenty-five more living without him, when I picked up the phone to call Ray I knew almost nothing about the pivotal experience that shaped our family.

Talking with Ray left me elated. That feeling continued as I followed up with the man he told me about in Connecticut who could add some pieces to the puzzle. It was easy enough to think back to the silence about such topics in our household. I also found myself thinking about my own complicity in that silence—first to keep the peace, but eventually to focus on my own life. Much of my curious lack of curiosity occurred after my father's death, when I couldn't have interrogated him anyway. But when did I first avert my gaze and focus instead on my own goals? At what age do we decide that our own future is much more interesting than our parents' past? Now, at least, I had a desire to know what had happened—and Ray was the best person to tell me.

I learned later, from another of the letters Dad wrote to Mom after the war, that Ray was a part of their lives even then. In a letter to "My Dearest Peg" written on the evening of June 7, 1947, my father describes a completely unexpected visit in Washington D.C. from his fellow waist gunner. Ray had been in New York with his new bride—it was, in fact, their honeymoon—when he suddenly decided they had to drive south to the nation's capital to see this guy he knew in the war. There is no mention of how his bride felt about the detour.

"Frankly, I was speechless," my father writes. He refers without explanation to "Ray Noury," suggesting that my mother already was familiar with the name. Perhaps she met him at some hospital or had heard my father speak of him. "After three and a half years, he hasn't changed, and it was grand to see him." The men's greatest regret, my father says, is that they couldn't be alone. Both my grandmother and Ray's wife were present, their presence keeping the conversation "general." "I still couldn't get over it," wrote my Dad. "He was surprised to hear of you and I being engaged." The former airmen did squeeze in some details of Miss Fortune's final flight, and almost surely of Ray's desperate fall to earth clutching a badly functioning parachute and (in some tellings) a crucifix. "From what he says, I would sacrifice everything to have been with him," writes my father, who had sacrificed so much in the skies above Germany already. "Things sure sounded fouled up." My father looked back at this edited version and promised my Mom, "I'll tell you just what he said when I see you."

As I would start to understand during my first phone call with him in 2013—and see clearly during my research over the months that followed—Ray had come into a time of some celebrity. By the final year of his life, he had made not one but two trips to the Czech Republic to take part in commemorations of his final crew. Essentially, all the villages around Nepomuk were thanking Ray for the ultimate price paid by his bomber mates that day in 1944, and by broader association, all the young men who had fought so valiantly to defeat the Nazis. And he'd found himself being interviewed by the media—both print and broadcast—any time there was a need for something about veterans of World War II.

I gathered that Ray's life had not been easy, before or after the war. For one thing, he was small—no matter what 5-foot-3 sounds like in theory, Ray seemed smaller than that. There wasn't an inch to spare inside a B-24, and looking at Ray made me wonder if he was made for such a tight space to fight a war. Most of all, by the time he became an object of attention in and around Woonsocket, R.I., he'd had plenty of time to ponder what his still being among the living might mean. "It's hard to figure out," he admitted to one reporter, sitting in his wheelchair with his wife Therese beside him. "Maybe there's a reason for it. I don't know." The more he thought about it, the less satisfying that answer seemed. "You have to figure there was a reason for it and it was my job to live life to the best that I could and have a family."

Ray's father had immigrated to the United States from Canada in 1922; Ray was born the next year. A native of Central Falls, R.I., Marie and Joseph Noury's son Ray was an eighteen-year-old getting paid eleven dollars a week to do what so many New Englanders had done for at least a century—work in a textile mill. His mother worked there too, with many other families and extended families. There were few avenues out of this life, and hearing about it shed more light on the limitations my parents talked about when they scrimped on themselves to pay for my education. And then, suddenly, there was a way out for the Ray Nourys of the world. The Nazis had overrun most of Europe, the Japanese were about to attack Americans at Pearl Harbor and FDR was about to declare ours a nation at war. Ray enlisted in the army not long after his father applied for and was denied naturalization as a United States citizen. Ray went from eleven dollars a week to twenty-one dollars a month after enlisting, and the military would carry him a long way from that mill.

Ray's first duties focused on spotting U-boats, the Nazi submarines that patrolled so much of the Atlantic sinking Allied ships. Even before there were American troops on these ships, there were

American weapons bound to England to help with the war effort. As Britain's Churchill and eventually America's Roosevelt understood, it was essential that we not let Britain fall to Hitler. We had to help the English survive long enough to let America build and draft and plan enough to enter directly into combat. Patrolling the Atlantic shipping lanes in a two-person airplane, it was Ray's job to scan in all directions for U-boats. When he sighted one, he would notify the Navy by radio so they could pursue it. One of Ray's surest memories of those days was seeing a U-boat on the ocean surface. He called it in, but he and his mate were under orders to leave the area before the situation was resolved.

Once the United States started the slow slog from North Africa into Nazi-occupied Sicily during the summer of 1943, Ray saw a path to be part of what clearly would be the Big Show. Everyone knew there was an invasion of Europe coming—though the D-Day Normandy invasion that would inspire the fateful Big Week of air attacks on German factories was still a closely guarded secret. Ray wanted to fly in the B-25 Mitchell, a quick twin-engine bomber that was more maneuverable than the vulnerable heavy bombers. But months of punishing crew losses over Europe meant the Army desperately needed replacements to fly on four-engine B-24s. Ray became one of them.

With his diminutive size, Ray was assigned to a waist gunner position where he fought back-to-back with another airman. The man who had Ray's back was my father. In any B-24 Liberator, the two gunners positioned here faced outward through a wide-open window, manning .50-caliber machine guns to fend off anyone who tried to shoot the plane down. When the attacks came— and they would, they learned in training—there would be only minutes, only seconds sometimes, to make a difference between coming back to base safely and becoming another casualty of war. What was the worst, to Ray, my Dad and just about anyone who flew, was that if you died doing this job, you helped cause the deaths of the guys counting on you. Your buddies. Your brothers.

With Ray's help, I began to piece together the life of the crew and Miss Fortune up until the December 1943 raid on Augsburg that ended combat for my father.

Ray's crucial role in explaining Miss Fortune's fate began many decades before I called him in 2013. Shortly after he returned to the United States in 1945, Ray wrote a long letter describing the crew's final mission to Regensburg. Ray wrote the letter to Grace Altemus, the wife of navigator Joe Altemus, who typed up copies and sent them to each of the crew families. When I obtained a copy of this letter several days after my initial telephone conversation with Ray, I felt like I had stumbled upon the Rosetta Stone. And as I later would learn first-hand, Grace Altemus was as much a part of Miss Fortune's story as Ray.

Ray's information was a first step for me towards understanding the long arc of a journey that began with the enlistment of individual crew members from all over the United States in 1941 and 1942. That arc continued through a training period that lasted well into 1943; the assembling of a B-24 crew and its arrival in Italy in late 1943; difficult missions deep into Germany in December 1943 and February 1944; and an agonizing period of limbo that lasted from February 1944 until mid-1945 as worried crew families clung to hope, exchanged frequent letters, and prayed while waiting to learn the fate of their missing husbands, sons and brothers.

Ray and other members of George Goddard's crew arrived in Europe after training in the Caribbean—including a brief sojourn in Cuba, popular at the time for its rum and fine cigars. According to Ray, the crew expected to fly from there to England, since that was what everybody did. Instead, they stopped off at Langley Field in Virginia to pick up my father. From there they flew via Greenland to Ireland—where their first plane was declared unfit to fly—and then on to Scotland. In a C-54 troop transport, they were flown to Marrakesh and then Casablanca in Morocco, the latter scene to several of the main Allied meetings that eventually led to Big Week. Once in Casablanca, they picked up another B-24 and readied themselves for combat.

Until the late fall of 1943, thanks to brave flying by the Eighth Air Force, the bombing of virtually anywhere in Nazi-occupied

Europe usually started out in England and, with luck, ended up there. Missions launched from England to attack Nazi positions across the Channel in France, or in Belgium or the Netherlands, were dangerous. The difficulty and casualty count increased tremendously when military planners began picking industrial targets inside Germany itself. Just getting to locations deep in Germany was challenge enough based on the bombers' fuel capacity and range. Tougher still were missions undertaken without fighter escort as pilots steered their lumbering bombers directly into the teeth of Luftwaffe units tasked with defending the Fatherland. The odds were stacked against crews directed to fly long distances into Germany and back through flak-filled skies swarming with deadly Messerschmitt fighters.

Italy remained a bloody quagmire, even after the Allies invaded in September 1943 and defeated Mussolini's homegrown troops. That only meant Nazis rushed in, and the fighting grew bloodier still. But as the Allies pushed even these battle veterans back toward the north, they opened up ground in their wake—ground from which Allied heavy bombers could take off using a series of hastily commissioned air bases in southern Italy. If crews could fly the length of Italy, clear the Alps, dodge the flak, survive the fighters and hit their factory targets, then their bombers could begin tearing the Nazi war machine apart within Germany itself.

As Ray, my father, and the rest of Goddard's crew soon discovered, Fifteenth Air Force bomber crews based in Italy received the same brutal Luftwaffe reception as their Eighth Air Force counterparts based in England. Ray succinctly summed up the crew's situation as they arrived overseas in late October 1943. "They were in need of crews on heavy bombers. So to Italy we went. From there on, [the] going was rough."

Knowing the crew's eventual fate even then, I asked Ray about their aircraft's prescient name. At one point, their assigned aircraft may have been named Butch by an earlier crew. Ray explained that there was some early talk among Goddard's crew of naming the plane Snow White, but apparently that never happened, never became official anyway. Ray liked Goddard's suggestion to name the aircraft Skipper after his unborn child. That never happened either.

And according to Ray, even the name Miss Fortune itself never gained official status as the moniker of this crew's plane—unlike another B-24 in the Eighth Air Force's 467th Bomb Group, based in England, which featured the same name painted with nose art.

Among Goddard's crew, however, the name Miss Fortune stuck. It wasn't that this unofficial nickname sounded especially hopeful, or that fliers in wartime weren't wracked by superstition, fear and a sense of impending doom every time their planes inched off the ground.. As I later would learn, Miss Fortune's crew nearly flew its final mission several times before Regensburg. The name was a grim joke and a nod to fate by airmen who quickly realized just how much luck they were going to need, and just how little there was to go around in late 1943.

"The name Miss Fortune was only in our memory—it was never put on," Ray would write later. "We thought the name suitable, not because we wanted it that way, but after being around so much it fitted us to perfection."

The near misses began on their layover in Greenland while heading overseas, when their plane nearly crashed on takeoff. The facts of their later missions after arriving in Italy only hint at the drama and the danger. On December 6, 1943, they bombed occupied Greece, doing the same to Sofia in Bulgaria four days later. Over the next few days, their assignments varied from Nazi positions still in Italy (Fiume on December 11 and Dogna on December 16) and a trip back to Greece to strike at Menidi in between. Those missions set the stage, though of course no one knew until the briefing that early morning, for a long haul to Augsburg on December 19. It would be the crew's first foray into the skies above Germany itself, and my father's last.

Goddard started one early mission as co-pilot but had to take over halfway through—over the bombing target, no less. On another early mission, they were given a new ship with superchargers—a new technology designed to boost engine power. High in the dangerous air, the superchargers failed and the plane dropped five thousand feet before Goddard was able to pull it out. On yet another mission, a propeller was hit by enemy fire and started "windmilling" faster than the propellers on the other three engines. "No control of it," Ray would recall, "and vibrating so badly that we were ready to bail out because we expected the propeller to come right off. We made a rough landing after going through a storm, but we made it back. The propeller came right off after we landed— luck was with us."

I wanted, in that initial phone conversation with Ray, to zero in on my father's wounding. It had become such as matter of faith for me, as it had for my mother during their courtship and early marriage, that here was the moment that changed his life. This was a kind of code, to be sure: Here was the moment that made him the sometimes silent, sometimes brooding, sometimes angry man we both knew and loved.

Ray told me more detail than I had anticipated. The flak exploded just underneath my Dad's firing position, Ray said, shearing the plane open like a can opener and imbedding countless metal fragments into his leg. Worse, perhaps, my father now had open air beneath him. Ray turned away from his .50-caliber and grabbed my father's parachute harness. Despite shrapnel wounds in his left arm and right shoulder, Ray dragged my father from their waist gun position near the tail along a narrow catwalk in the bomb bay toward the plane's cockpit. Only in the cramped quarters immediately behind the cockpit could he force his crewmate to inhale reviving oxygen, and wipe and bind his shredded leg. Then came the hours-long flight back to their base in Brindisi (if indeed they could reach it) before my father bled to death. The freezing air at nearly twenty-five thousand feet helped to slow the blood loss. I later learned that Ray was awarded the Distinguished Flying Cross for his actions during the Aubsburg mission when he saved my father. George Goddard submitted the paperwork shortly after that mission, and the medal was waiting for Ray when he returned from his POW ordeal in 1945. But Ray did not accept the medal until 2002. Ray himself never mentioned it to me.

The point Ray emphasized, which I saw referenced in the sortie report and other documents, was that my father stuck to his gun position after he was hit and kept firing until he downed an attacking ME 110 fighter. "Don't know how he ever stood the strain and pain," Ray said. "What a guy, what courage."

In one phone call, Ray had answered my burning question: What was the "something bad" that had happened to my father? I had wondered about this question since childhood, when I would sneak into my parents' room while my father was at work; remove the box containing his Purple Heart from his dresser; open the lid; and hold it in my hand while trying to figure out why the man coming home for dinner at six had a heart-shaped medal in his sock drawer. His medal topped the list of things not to talk about.

As I digested Ray's information during the days that followed, my initial elation began to ebb. I now knew details about item number one on William D. Boyce's Do Not Ask List. But I began to grasp that the list of things I wanted to know was vastly longer than I had imagined. The search was not over. It had hardly begun.

Identifikační známky čtyř členů posád

DOG TAGS RECOVERED FROM THE CRASH SITE.

CHAPTER THREE

THE TAIL GUNNER'S NEPHEW

S hortly before Ray and I said our goodbyes and ended our first phone conversation, he gave me a name and contact information for another man who would prove to be invaluable in my quest for information. There was a man in Connecticut, John Torrison, who had been researching that last flight for some years and who had pulled together a lot of varied bits and pieces. John had twice been to the villages in what was now the Czech Republic, accompanying Ray to the annual commemorations. John was a nephew of Wayne Nelson, one of the ten Americans who died on the hillside that day.

It took only minutes chatting with John on the phone to sense his passion for the subject, although I sometimes wondered why. Nelson had perished before John had even been born, so there was so direct or personal relationship between uncle and nephew. In fact, John let on, his only solid feeling of relation came from a painting his grandmother kept of her son in uniform and the briefest report that he had been killed in World War II. Starting with only those limited strands, John had turned himself into a research machine—something that propelled him to the limits of family genealogy and military history. Though much of his work over almost a decade was done by computer, I had the distinct impression that John combined the finer qualities of a news reporter and a private detective, pounding the pavement and tirelessly knocking on doors. Over the years, the doors started to open for John Torrison.

John knew how to capture my interest. Within days of our hanging up, he had emailed a copy of Ray's June 1945 letter entitled, "Our Last Mission." This was the letter Ray sent to navigator Joe Altemus's wife, Grace, who in turn typed it and distributed it to the crew families. It's really two letters rolled into one. The first half talks about the crew's last mission to Regensburg from briefing-room dread to their desperate last moments before falling from the sky on February 22, 1944. The second half talks about each of the crew members and the crew's history leading up to their fatal final mission.

Time and time again, John Torrison felt himself carried back to the 1945 letter. As much as he hoped he could track down surviving family members, he understood that by the new millennium those were getting fewer and farther between. And quite frankly, the memories of those who remained were likely to be getting vague. Ray's telling of the story while still a young man spurred John to learn more and provided a roadmap of where to look.

With the immediacy of these conversations and this letter, the past began to come into better focus for me. John's life and mission became another piece I felt compelled to understand, even as my own personal search for the source of my father's volatility moved forward with his help. Who was John Torrison, really? And why had he devoted so much of his life to finding out the truth about a relative he'd never met? By way of answer, I have only what John told me when I met him and his older brother George face-to-face: "I felt like there was a hole in our family." I knew exactly what he meant.

Thanks to his parents' upward mobility, John grew up in a series of Chicago suburbs, as did I. Yet his roots lay among the strong-willed Scandinavian stock on a Wisconsin farming town called Valders. That's where his parents, Hartley and Lola, had been raised, and it seems they raised John and his siblings in the spirit of a Valders childhood. Indeed, small town relationships played a role in their meeting, since Lola left Valders to take a job previously held by Hartley's older sister as a maid for a railroad executive near Chicago.

John first became aware of his deceased Uncle Wayne during summer visits to his grandmother's house back in Valders. He was six or seven when he noticed a painting of Wayne Nelson hanging next to the couch in the home's small sitting room. For years, he thought that Uncle Wayne had died when his plane crashed in Germany.

"I felt he was important," John told me. "I had never seen a painting of someone in our family. I felt a sense of sadness and pride. But frankly, I was in my own world and felt like WWII was like ancient history. I don't remember ever talking about Wayne or the war's effect on my parents' families with anyone."

John's older brother, George, was about ten when their uncle Wayne left to go overseas. George remembered a quiet young man who was an avid reader, and who thought his given name "Wayneworth" was a bit too stiff and formal. He preferred to be called "Ole." George remembered Wayne's last visit home during summer 1943, and a picture of Wayne at a family gathering in Valders during the visit with a bratwurst in one hand and a beer in the other. George also remembered the scene when his mother found out that Wayne was missing in action. "She couldn't hardly stand it," George said, "and had to go outside for a walk to calm down." Lola never talked much about Wayne in her later years, but she always honored his memory.

For John, the desire to know took hold after he had grown up, married and taken a career of his own. By the time his last Nelson uncle passed away in 1998, all of his parents' fourteen brothers and sisters were gone. Lola and Hartley had outlived their siblings but were drifting rapidly into dementia. Soon, John understood, there would be no one left on earth to ask.

When John started to clean out his folks' home in Florida he stumbled on scrapbooks with more information, including the simple truth that Wayne's brothers Walter and Russell both were commissioned officers. Walter graduated from the University of Wisconsin at Madison and entered the Navy as an ensign in May 1943. Russell entered the Army Air Forces and later graduated from Pepperdine University of the GI Bill. John's attention was captured by a combination of photos from that time and Ray's letter that Grace had forwarded to his grandmother. John and George contacted Ray for the first time in August 2001, between the deaths of their mother and then their father. They paid their first visit to Ray in Rhode Island less than a year after that. "It started to become real to me," John recalls of those days, "an unknown part of my family history."

WAYNE NELSON, ROBERT TORRISON, RUSSELL NELSON, GEORGE TORRISON AND FAMILY FRIEND BILLY CRYSTAL IN VALDERS, WISCONSIN DURING THE SUMMER OF 1943.

Early on, John spent a good deal of time reading and re-reading Ray's first-hand account; after meeting Ray in 2002, John studied four photographs in Ray's possession that were taken of the crew on February 15, 1944. The impossibly young men just days away from Miss Fortune's last mission were laughing and smiling, though in Ray's clear-eyed narrative they did neither on the morning they heard Regensburg was their destination. The first photo showed Lt. George Goddard and his co-pilot, 2nd Lt. Haig Kandarian, while the second showed the plane's bombardier, 2nd Lt. Charles Spickard, and 2nd Lt. Joe Altemus. Next came a group photo with Ray grinning as he wrapped his arm around John's uncle, tail gunner Wayne Nelson, whom Ray invariably called "Lord Nelson." Next stood Harold Carter from Illinois, then crew chief Melvin Adams from Maryland and finally Roy E. Hughes from Texas.

Staff Sgt. John Goldbach was not in any of the photos. Goldbach had replaced my father aboard Miss Fortune after his wounding over Augsburg two months earlier.

I later would learn that Mel Adams missed Miss Fortune's last mission on February 22, 1944 because he was grounded for medical reasons at the last minute. Staff Sgt. Oscar Houser took his place. Being grounded before the last mission, which might look like a lucky break to an outsider, tormented Mel Adams for the rest of his life.

There were all my father's crewmates, however, standing and kneeling in one final photo beside their B-24. Goddard and Kandarian had their eyes closed when the camera shutter clicked.

I had discovered a copy of the crew's final photo in an old photo album years before I connected with John. It meant little to me without names and context. John provided both when he forwarded the Ray-Grace letter of June 1945. More questions were answered. And more were raised, too.

Some of my new questions focused on Grace Altemus. Who was she, and how did she fit into the story? John began filling me in. He had corresponded with Grace for a decade and visited her in person as part of his own dogged investigation. He was intrigued to learn that Grace and Joe Altemus had been married only a month before Joe flew off to war in late 1943. And the more John learned about Grace, the more he became transported to another time and place.

Joe Altemus was working as one of the hundreds of draftsmen employed by Bethlehem Steel in Pennsylvania when he first laid eyes on the "steno" named Grace Malloy. Grace was one of the only females in the place, and even more importantly, she was the one passing out timecards to the workers each morning. She remembers noticing Joe but not paying him any special attention until he returned from officer's training in uniform. "He humbled me, and we were engaged that night," Grace told John.

Once overseas, Joe became one of the thousands of GIs who conspired to tell their loved ones where they were in ways agreed upon in advance. "He wrote me using the first initial of the country they went to as my middle initial," Grace said. "So I learned they were in Italy." In one letter, Joe even talked about a conversation he'd had with another fellow in the unit. After Joe answered the question "Where are you from?" one listener said the only girl he ever knew in Bethlehem was Grace Malloy. Joe was able to respond proudly, "I just married her."

When Miss Fortune was shot down in February 1944, Grace the stenographer became Grace the correspondent. She wrote frequently to the crew families and became a one-woman information clearinghouse as they worried and waited to find out what had happened. One of Grace's many letters went to Wayne Nelson's mother, found its way into John Torrison's hands, and eventually landed in my inbox.

After more than three years of hard fighting, Americans had reason to hope the war's end was in sight by June 1945. While no one doubted that the price to invade Japan would be high, the fighting in Europe had ended. Germany's surrender meant that Ray could come home. He stayed in Rhode Island through August; at Grace's request, he put in writing what he had told her as soon as he was back on American soil.

The typewritten version of this June 1945 letter includes a preamble by Grace that begins, "Dear Crew Members." She explained that she was relaying the letter Ray had written to her. "I hate passing it on to you," Grace wrote, "just as Ray Noury must have hated writing it, but you are probably just as anxious to know the facts as I was. Ray called me when he got in and told me some of this and then I asked him to put it down in writing. I couldn't write you about the phone call because I was afraid I didn't have the correct information. I am grateful to Ray for his courage."

Beginning his narration, Ray insisted he still couldn't believe that only he had survived among "such a great bunch of fellows." He admitted to Grace: "I have been trying for the past ten days but just couldn't put it down." Recalling the details of the crew's last mission to Grace Altemus not long after Hitler killed himself and Germany surrendered, Ray summed up the story he'd lived to tell by describing his crew with four simple words: "Faithful to the end."

Ray's letter understandably spends less time talking about the December 19, 1943 attack on Augsburg than about Miss Fortune's February 22, 1944 attack on Regensburg. That makes sense because he was gathering whatever facts he had and his own recollections for the widow of a crew member who died that day. In fact, he doesn't even talk of saving my Dad's life. To hear him tell it this time out, he and Bill Boyce were wounded in the bombing run and hospitalized afterward, my father to be treated in Italy, then sent to a better medical facility in Africa and finally home, Ray to return to his bombing mates. What he does talk about is the nightmare over Augsburg—surely for those who read his letter, the nightmare before the final nightmare.

The thirty-four bombers on the Augsburg mission were sent off without a fighter escort—no "little friends," as the bomber crews often called them—perhaps because the fighters lacked the range for a long trek over the Alps to Germany. Once they neared Augsburg, however, they ran into lots of enemies. As many as 150 Messerschmitts swarmed around the bombers from above, below and any possible angle. Ray and my Dad went to work from Miss Fortune's midsection, firing their .50-calibers as carefully as could be expected of very young men facing death at such close range.

"Nearly all of us looked like a Swiss cheese," offered Ray, letting on that six or seven of the American bombers were shot down over Augsburg that day. "Don't know how we made it back, but we did."

Ray was treated for shrapnel wounds in a combat hospital after Augsburg, sitting out a mission or two—meaning that his crewmates had to fly over enemy territory with both waist gunner positions filled by strangers. Airmen hated few things more than flying combat missions with guys they didn't know. That was instant bad luck.

January 1944 was an important month around the crew's airbase in southern Italy. There were twenty to twenty-five missions taking off, yet somewhat to Ray's apparent disappointment, these did not involve Goddard's crew. "The best month of all went to waste," he later wrote, referring to the operational training ordered for them. "Here we were putting in seventy-five hours on borrowed time." It's a near-certainty that Ray chose those final few words in light of all that took place in February.

At the start of that month, the crew went on "flak leave" in Bari, just over seventy miles up the Italian coast. Typically, all fighting men loved when they were granted leave, but all the talk from Ray was about how little there was to do and especially how little there was to eat. I was reminded, listening to him as well as reading his letter, of my father's response decades earlier that he and his buddies weren't in Italy to eat pizzas. "Italy is poor. It's pitiful," Ray wrote to Grace Altemus. "Only wish I could have bought more for our Little Skipper." Goddard's unborn child had already become the crew's special mascot, perhaps also a kind of much-prized good luck charm. "George was so proud and so were we. He got a razzing from all of us quite often, but he took it swell."

Ray Noury's final days as waist gunner aboard Miss Fortune were busy ones. The crew returned from Bari on February 9 and, according to Ray's recollections, had its first mission the next morning, followed by one on February 15 and another on February 19. That

CHARLES SPICKARD AND JOE ALTEMUS PHOTOGRAPHED ON FEBRUARY 15, 1944.

last one was both terrible and terrifying, flying in and out of so much flak that the plane returned full of holes. As was procedure, these had to be patched up, forcing cancellation of another mission the very next day. The predawn of February 22 arrived after a night of poor sleep for many who would fly aboard Miss Fortune.

"I guess we all feel something strange or some little incident whenever things are apt to go wrong," Ray wrote in his letter to Grace. "Well, that morning I felt it inside. Of course, it was only after everything happened that they came to me. After briefing at the Intelligence Office, usually George, Kandy, Spic [Spickard] and Joe arrived at the plane together, but that morning Joe was by himself. Joe told us that the target was Regensburg, the furthest point ever hit in Germany by the 15th Air Force, and before we had a chance to say anything George called us together."

"'Boys, it's Regensburg and you can expect the worst. No fighter escort so keep your guns working and your eyes open at all times. Check them often and report if anything goes wrong. Okay, check them before we kick off." Ray recounted this was the first time he'd ever seen Goddard appear nervous, and he wondered if it had something to do with his unborn "Little Skipper" back in the States, whom he had never seen and indeed would never see.

GEORGE GODDARD AND HAIG KANDARIAN ON FEBRUARY 15, 1944.

John Torrison was not the first Nelson family member to seek answers from Ray. About two years after John and I first communicated, John sent me another letter in which Ray was front and center. This January 1947 letter was from John's grandmother—Wayne's mother, Sophia Nelson. She starts out by thanking Ray for sending her a Christmas card; she then peers straight into the "hole in our family" that John himself would come to recognize years later. Christmas is the time when "one looks and waits for every one in the family to be home," Mrs. Nelson tells Ray. That could not happen for her after Wayne's death: "Never heard any more [from him]...only just—missing." She continues, "Jan. 25th is Wayne's birthday. [O]nly thing I can do is to remember him in my prayers. [N]o other gift can I give him."

Mrs. Nelson asked Ray if he could give her any information about the crew's crash location or "where they could have landed" because a "young fellow in [t]he Service" who "lives across the street from us" was scheduled to ship out for Germany soon. "I would like very much to have this Boy go and look around and see if he could not find some trace of some thing or inquire around.... And he would be glad to do it."

Two of the other remarkable documents John Torrison uncovered in his research concerned my father in the first few months of his hospitalization. Not only do they provide additional information—a fact here, an impression there—but they also reflect the flurry of letter-writing that no doubt followed the loss of many young men to the horrors of war. They show, in particular, the efforts to maintain the correct balance of hope and cold reality when no one is saying, officially or otherwise, whether the loved one is fine, wounded, a prisoner of war or simply dead.

The crew families grew increasingly anxious when the letters stopped coming from overseas after February 22, 1944. Anxiety turned to dread when they received telegrams in March 1944 officially notifying them that their husbands, sons and brothers were "missing in action"—a cruelly ambiguous status hanging somewhere between life and death, optimism and despair, that would continue well into 1945. The families filled much of their time by exchanging letters with one another; the encouragement they had poured into words headed for Italy was redirected stateside to spouses, parents and siblings suffering through the same punishing uncertainty. Any scrap of news or speculation was reason enough to write. And, it turns out that Peggy Lesko was not the only person who made a pilgrimage to Cleveland to see my father in hopes of gaining information about the crew.

On April 28, 1944, Grace Altemus typed out a two-page, single-space letter to "Dear Mrs. Nelson," John's grandmother, whose son Wayne was listed as missing along with Grace's husband Joe after the Regensburg raid. Even more intriguingly, the reason behind the letter seems to be Grace's just-completed and rather tiring train trip to visit my Dad at Crile General Hospital in Cleveland. While he was not part of the crew that was lost, he was such an indelible link to the group that Grace invariably calls "the boys" that she felt it worth the difficult travel. She makes a point of telling Mrs. Nelson she got back to Bethlehem the night before she had to return to work at 8:30 a.m.

"He's a fine lad and is crazy about the crew," Grace wrote of my father. "He didn't mind being wounded and having himself laid up as much as he minded being wounded and leaving the boys." The hospital itself, she recounted, was very comfortable and was essentially state-of-the-art for 1944, having just been dedicated on the day she started on her train journey there. "All the boys are wonderful—they're just all anxious to get out and back in the fight again."

Having heard details of the December 19 mission to Augsburg directly from my father, Grace showed the same reverence for a first-hand account she would show for Ray Noury's letter in 1945. Miss Fortune had just dropped its bombs on Augsburg when a "Jerry fighter" (in the wartime lingo of that time) shot at the side of the plane, which meant directly at my father. According to this retelling, a 20 mm shell exploded directly beside my father, but he kept on firing his .50-caliber until he shot down the plane. Only afterward, Grace recounted, once the plane had flown into relative safety and met up with some American fighters, did my father notice how badly he was wounded. "Bill looked at his leg," she wrote, weaving in details that had to come from later medical examination and treatment. "Well, it was sticking out in three different directions and there were 100 pieces of shrapnel throughout."

It's strange sometimes, reading Grace's letter about my father so many decades later—decades during which so many things about the war were left unsaid in my life. In writing about a tragedy that changed her own life so completely, she was also writing about the tragedy that defined my childhood. "He is a wonderful person," wrote Grace of the man I struggled to know, "modest and unassuming. He's direct and soft-spoken. You will like him on sight. The best thing about him is his sincere liking for all the rest—they're always in his thoughts."

In reading Grace's letter I noticed that its account of my father's wounding differed from Ray's account delivered to me over the telephone. Ray attributed the explosion and resulting wound to a flak burst. Grace's letter recounts that a 20 mm shell detonated next to my father's leg after being fired from an attacking fighter.

The difficulty in determining exactly what happened illustrated for me the importance and uncertainty of relying on old memories and old letters. Which is the better source—an account from a living eyewitness whose recollections may have dimmed during the course of seven decades, or one from a long-dead eyewitness that was told to and then retold by a correspondent? From my vantage point, I was hungry for any information and grateful that so many letters survived for so long. The time-consuming practice of writing letters, long since swallowed up by more immediate and casual forms of electronic communication, allowed at least fleeting glimpses into the events of 1943 and 1944. An inhabitant of our current hyperconnected age may have difficulty imagining wives, children and parents going months and sometimes a year or more without knowing the fate of loved ones in the military. Writing to Wayne's mother, Grace expressed the hope that, even though things didn't look good, their "boys" somehow made it to the ground safely and were prisoners of war (like they would learn Ray Noury had been) or were perhaps even safe but out of contact in ever-neutral Switzerland.

One of the parts of Grace's letter that touched me most was my father's warm memories of the way he and his friends enjoyed being together when they weren't on a mission—many practical jokes—leading up to the way they cared for him after he was hit. George Goddard, he told Grace, even landed the B-24 extra gently so my Dad wouldn't feel any more pain than necessary. I was touched by his sensitivity describing his war buddies, feared to be dead, to this worried wife. Talking at the hospital, he managed to tell Grace Altemus the thing she found "most consoling" up to that point in the long wait.

"He told me that he saw those boys when they were in actual combat—when they were surrounded by the enemy—and he told me how cool they were," Grace wrote Mrs. Nelson, moving from consoled to consoler. "It wasn't that they weren't scared or that they were brave. But they all had so much to them—and they were so well trained—that they did what was expected of them and more." The hope clearly lived on. "He told me that no matter what happened on Feb. 22nd that they knew what to do."

The second letter, penned by "Dear Mrs. Nelson" only six days later to her daughter Lola (John Torrison's mother), incorporated the news that Grace Altemus had written of her visit with my Dad in Cleveland plus an extended passage he had written separately to her about the crew. To my modern eyes, the transition in Mrs. Nelson's handwriting from one narrator to the other at first seemed odd, but I realized it was only a manual version of what Grace would do by typewriter with Ray Noury's letter the following year. It was the only way for people to share letters and information in the days before photocopiers and emails. Reading the letter felt like eavesdropping on a conversation.

My father went to some lengths to use Ray Noury's survival as reason to hope that others aboard may still be alive and well. He insisted that he knew "from personal experience" that the boys had many ways to escape the fate that all were fearing by this point, that almost certainly more than one "got out" and that it would be only a matter of time before the families received some hopeful news from Europe.

In one final flourish, he talked about the courageous role Mrs. Nelson's son Wayne played on December 19 when he was wounded. He shared the truth that without hard fighting aboard Miss Fortune the end may have come much sooner than we now know it did. "I don't have to tell you how good a fellow Wayne is, just as straight and honest a fellow as they come," my father wrote, being careful to use the present tense. "The way he stuck by his guns on that eventful Sunday—we owe everything to him for that."

While the accounts of the families' fears and questions brought up one set of emotions, the experience of Ray as the known survivor stirred up others. Like many of the newspaper and broadcast reporters who interviewed Ray late in his life, John Torrison was fascinated by the bizarre tale of his survival—being blown or tossed from Miss Fortune as it started to rip apart in midair, falling fifteen thousand feet with a parachute that worked only marginally, and, of course, landing in that snowdrift. Early on, Ray and John never talked much about what happened after Ray was captured; that changed when Ray was interviewed for a possible movie about POWs. John would take a particular interest in "Ray's War," especially his time as a POW.

John was able to videotape a full six hours of interviews at Ray's house in Rhode Island. As is common in recollections from so long ago, the conversations sometimes ramble, but they do offer a highly personal view. Most strikingly, Ray's narrative does not describe the proud and disciplined Germany that marched across Europe early in the war, seemingly unstoppable. We really do see something more akin to fugitives from a massive manhunt, ducking and digging in until it was time to run again. With effort, triangulating with the help of a few historic events, John was able to construct a timeline of Ray's experiences from the day in February 1944 when he found himself in German hands until his liberation by the advancing American forces shortly before the Reich's official end in May 1945. It begins in late February 1944 with a few days of intense interrogation at the Durchgangslager der Luftwaffe (Transit Camp of the Luftwaffe) created for that purpose few miles northwest of Frankfurt.

"I don't remember how I got there," Ray told John's video camera. "I guess it was by train. We went all the way to Frankfurt,

Germany, under the Gestapo…To my amazement the captain of the Gestapo spoke very good English. He had been educated somewhere in this country, somewhere in Ohio…[There were] all kinds of questions about where you were born and try to get to your parents, and all the time they knew. They were trying to get you to tell them a little more, in hopes that you may tell them a little more than they already had…Tell us what you know. They wanted to know how many planes we had."

Though Ray doesn't specifically say whether he had such training, these far-ranging interrogations at the interrogation camp had inspired a specific course of study within the American military. The United States leadership had been told of the constant questioning by psychologists, usually over one or two weeks but sometimes close to a month. Prisoners of war were studied closely to determine their mental state and emotional tendencies. Were they more likely to provide important information in response to fear, for instance, or in return for special luxuries? If no particular weakness was uncovered, the prisoners here were not physically tortured but were placed for long periods in solitary confinement. At the very least, this was a punishment; at the most, it was another chance to crack the prisoner's will to resist. The American training sought to prepare servicemen for such treatment with information, and to stress the high cost to fellow GIs in the past when the wrong piece of information slipped out. From this training the now-famous practice of giving only name, rank and serial number emerged.

The 500-acre camp and its intelligence-gathering mission both were important to the Nazi plan as the war entered its later phase. No longer possessing men or material to fight anywhere anytime, especially after the air attacks on factories in cities like Augsburg and Regensburg, the Nazis had no choice but to fight smarter. And knowing that American bombers from England and eventually Italy were passing overhead or nearby, they formed the words "Prisoner of War Camp" with white rocks on the grass and white paint on the roofs of buildings. The greatest interrogation center in all of Europe, which questioned virtually every Allied airman taken prisoner on the continent, was left alone by the bombers.

While the plan was always to move POWs like Ray from the interrogation center to a standard camp, even the transfer introduced Ray to the descending chaos that would be Germany from that point forward. On his way with "a lot of prisoners from everywhere," Ray faced the danger of death from the sky every bit as much as death on the ground. "They kept picking them up," Ray told John of the train journey, "and the British hit Frankfurt that night. They had to get us out of the boxcars and run us to their underground. And if you want to know how scary it is when you get these bombs coming down, I'll tell you it is very scary. I hadn't been in many situations like this." It's worth noting that even a member of bomber crew who fell from his plane as it disintegrated found the experience of being bombed the stuff of lifelong nightmares.

As far as anyone can determine, Ray's next stop began and ended shortly before the location made its way into World War II legend, with the help of books and at least one high-profile movie. Ray apparently spent less than a month in East Prussia at Stalag III Luft. Ray remembers fellow prisoners digging some sort of tunnel underneath the stove and slipping the dirt and stones they removed into their pockets to toss into the latrine when they were allowed to go. That way the Germans didn't notice anything suspicious. History and Hollywood would record the events that followed, perhaps only days after Ray was moved elsewhere, in a 1963 movie called *The Great Escape.*

He did have memories of the camp, however. It was his introduction to life as a *Kriegie,* short for the German word for prisoner of war, *kriegsgefangenen.* By this point in the war, Germany was running out of food and other necessities for its own fighting men, so it certainly didn't have any to spare for the enemy. Stories come down through various written accounts of "green death soup," a disgusting cooked-down mishmash of rotting vegetables, and its next of kin "gray death," water mixed with uncooked flour. Lice were a constant problem, and the guards gave the prisoners nothing to combat them.

No significant medical attention was given to Ray at this camp or at any of the ones that followed. He'd been quickly examined and given what amounted to first aid by the Germans who picked him up shortly after he landed and after that, anything resembling surgery would have been a luxury. According to Ray, the Germans didn't know he had broken his neck in the fall. Ray didn't either until X-rays taken some sixty years later revealed a healed fracture in a vertebra.

Because the American air assault had not gotten serious by the time Stalag III Luft opened in 1942, the original mission had been to house British airmen. That would soon change—not least after the heavy losses encountered by Miss Fortune and other American crews during Big Week. Only months before Ray's arrival from the interrogation center, a special South Compound had been opened for American airmen, keeping them separate from the North Compound for British flyers, from which The Great Escape was staged. Before long, Stalag III Luft grew to sixty acres, housing about 2,500 Royal Air Force officers, nearly 7,500 members of the U.S. Army Air Corps and about 900 men from a collection of other Allies.

There was considerable value assigned to being an airman at the stalag. For one thing, the guards were Luftwaffe personnel (too old, too young or too wounded for combat) so there was a level of respect, at least man to man, not found in most other, mixed-population German POW camps. For another thing, a huge effort was made to keep these prisoners alive—while going to all possible lengths to keep them from escaping. It was so clear that the bombing raids were cutting off the lifeblood of the Third Reich that the camp feared an airman finding his way back to the Allies would be back aloft dropping bombs on Germany within days.

From Stalag Luft III, Ray was moved by train and cattle truck to Stalag Luft IV in Pomerania, a long-disputed area along the Baltic Sea to the east. Germany claimed Pomerania as its own after centuries of settlement and development, but Poland claimed the region too. If the motive for the move was to get the POWs farther away from the American and British troops approaching from the west, by early 1945, the Germans faced the opposite problem. The Soviet army was approaching from the east, and by near-universal belief, its soldiers were more vicious to captives than any other. Ray had been a prisoner of war for just short of a year when the now-infamous Death March began in early 1945.

Temperatures remained below freezing and snow covered the ground, Ray remembered. The trek that, in segments, would keep him on the move the rest of the war began with a single step from his barracks at Stalag Luft IV into the devastating cold. Combining prisoners from the various camps, more than eighty thousand prisoners were forced to march westward over several routes across Poland, Czechoslovakia and Germany. They were joined, in a punishing journey that covered 500 more miles, by thousands of German men, women and children, all intent to flee the atrocities of the Red Army. In all, upwards of 3,500 American and Allied prisoners would die of disease and exposure to the elements during the march. As he had survived the crash of Miss Fortune, Ray Noury lived through this next harrowing challenge, too.

"We started at the camp," he remembered. "There was a good foot of snow when we left the camp. They had emplacements in the woods with dogs and everything. I guess they were trying to get us to make a run for it. We were keeping quiet. The head one said 'Keep cool,' just let them in, don't get out of line...They were having a tough time. They were evacuating for a reason."

While conditions were awful for travel on foot, not least in a large group of refugees across terrain that had long ago been stripped of food or anything else useful, Ray had one consolation. He understood what the march meant. Back at the stalag, a British soldier had kept a secret radio that allowed him to pick up regular news broadcasts. He was able to explain to Ray and his fellow prisoners that the Germans were on the run, initially from the Americans but then, as the end neared, back toward the Americans to escape the Russians. Germans and Allies alike could think of no better option than to surrender into the care of the red, white and blue.

One of Ray's most memorable events during the Death March was being taken to the port city called Swinemunde by the Germans (or Swinoujscie by the Polish) and loaded onto a dilapidated ship. The reason for this was unclear. In his last years, Ray was unsure about where the ship was trying to take him and wondered whether the prisoners had been placed there in hopes that they would be killed by mistake in a bombing attack. But he never forgot the misery of being packed into a dark, airless ship's hold with about a thousand other prisoners, many suffering from vomiting and diarrhea. He and some other small guys used their belts to suspend themselves above the crowd, thus giving the other guys as much space as possible. After several days of apparently sailing nowhere, the POWs were ordered to disembark.

"The Americans could have blown us up, right in the harbor... Then they decided there's no way they can get us anywhere, so they took us out, then they took us out through the woods, with a gun emplacement this time. There was no snow then and they handcuffed us one leg to each guy and one arm to each guy. We had to run in cadence. Thank goodness we knew that. So whoever it was the head one, I told him make sure you keep your mind focused...I guess we must have lost quite a few hundred men."

There were several theories, especially after Germany's surrender meant its officers could be questioned, about why Hitler ordered the final Death March. In the moment, many of the marchers feared they were being directed toward concentration camps for extermination—since rumors of what had happened to thousands (and ultimately millions) of Jews had already become part of the conversation. While certainly at odds with the Geneva Convention, such a move was seen as the Fuhrer's revenge for the Allies targeting civilians in their bombing runs, specifically during the fire-bombing of Dresden. Many German officers, however, insisted the goal was to keep the prisoners alive and use them as hostages in the seemingly inevitable peace negotiations. It was in that circumstance, they insisted, that Hitler considered executing as many of thirty-five thousand POWs if his demands were not being met. He did not live to make any such demands.

With Americans closing in on one side and Russians on the other—Ray insisted he could hear the armies moving closer—the prisoners were at last forced to head south. They covered more than 500 miles deep into Bavaria, all the while wondering why their German captors didn't simply give up. Thanks to the convergence of eighty thousand prisoners from many nations and many different branches of service, Stalag VIIA in Moosburg ended up being Germany's largest POW camp of the war. Moosburg (first mentioned under a different name in the year 879) is sometimes noted as the oldest settlement between Italy, where Miss Fortune took off, and Regensburg, the target of its final, fateful mission.

Within the gates of Stalag VIIA, Ray Noury's long, painful wartime pilgrimage came to an end. He was liberated by American forces reaching the camp on April 29, 1945.

GRACE ALTEMUS RECEIVES JOE ALTEMUS'S AIR MEDAL.

CHAPTER FOUR
SAVING GRACE

On St. Patrick's Day 1944, Grace Altemus received the telegram that changed her life.

Working at Bethlehem Steel as she had been before meeting Joe Altemus, she now waited for word from him or about him as he fought for his country in Europe. He had been there several months, mostly in an Italy recently liberated from the Third Reich, and he and Grace wrote each other two or even three times a day. In recent weeks, the letters from overseas had slowed to a trickle and then stopped. Grace was at the steel plant that terrible morning when her father arrived without warning, bearing an official government telegram. Joe, who had been her husband for only a month before shipping out, was listed as Missing in Action.

As a young bride, Grace may not have known what to do with the rest of her life after Joe Altemus was declared missing and then, a year later, declared dead. Yet she found her mission at the very heart of this loss, knowing from personal experience how families of other crew members must feel.

I was impressed with Grace Altemus from the moment John emailed me a scan of her letter after we hung up the phone. Her courage came through her short but committed introduction: here were the facts about our loved ones' demise, we don't want to hear them or know them or accept them, but we need to because, somehow, they would have wanted us to. Grace struck me as a card-carrying member of The Greatest Generation, a twenty-three-year-old woman who deeply loved her new husband, who mourned him as many years as her heart demanded, and who persevered. She remarried in 1949 and went on to raise three sons. At the same time, she was a little different. Unlike many women who joined the labor force in the Rosie the Riveter era, Grace had been working in a tough, male-dominated industry in a tough, male-dominated town long before the "boys" started heading off to Europe or the Pacific.

Somewhere along the way, she and second husband Reginald M. "Bud" Hodgson, Jr. had moved from Bethlehem, Pennsylvania, to Cocoa Beach, Florida. And that was where John finally paid her a visit after several years of exchanging a remarkable collection of emails. John's dinner with Grace was both unforgettable and surprisingly ordinary.

"Her home was one of those one-story Florida 'ranch' homes with a lanai on the back near the boat dock and waterway," John said. "It was similar to my folks' Florida home on Bird Key in Sarasota, except theirs was not on the waterway. Even some of the furniture was similar to my folks', and the dinner of Safeway baked chicken with macaroni and cheese was like my mother's idea of cooking in her final years."

As John recalled, Grace's husband (whom she and everybody else called Buddy) was slipping at the time into senility, a fact that sent him off to bed as soon as the dishes were cleared. That left John and Grace alone to talk about The Crew—about Joe, naturally, and Ray and also Skipper Goddard, the pilot's daughter.

Encountering Grace after such a happy marriage to Bud, John was surprised by how much she continued to love Joe. They spoke of reading, which they both loved, and of the Brevard Watercolor Society, which she founded to brighten the world with art. "We talked of her life now and her sons and her little dog, who'd gotten loose when she first opened the door for me," said John. "It was a wonderful time that I'll never forget. I think it was an important part of her life that she was revisiting and finally found peace."

The more fascinated I became with Grace herself, the more resonance I came to feel when reading through the emails she and John exchanged beginning in 2004. At first glance, I was amazed and admiring that a woman who worked at a steel mill in the early 1940s and suffered the tragedies of World War II had embraced this new technology with such gusto. Yet Grace had, using it with the same manners and style she had poured onto paper in what now seemed a lost world.

Knowing that Grace had visited my father at Crile General Hospital early in his treatment and recuperation there, I suppose I was looking primarily for insights about him. My mission remained a better understanding of the father this man became, and I couldn't shake the belief or fear that he had started becoming that man on December 19, 1943. Still, I quickly realized, Grace's focus on her husband and John's on his uncle meant that narratives regarding my father were few and far between. "I remember taking a train there," she writes of her visit to my father, "and going to see him but he really could tell me nothing more than I already knew. We didn't keep in touch."

Although this lack of information sent me back into the void that I so often felt when thinking of my father, like John Torrison, I found myself wanting to know more about the others whose lives this tragedy affected. Moving passages of Grace's emails throughout those early months of 2004 described her falling in love with Joe Altemus. By Grace's own reckoning, she was the only woman working among as many as 250 men, most of them young, fit and single. Many of them asked her out on dates, including trips to Philadelphia to dance the night away with Glenn Miller and Cab Calloway. Grace loved to dance, even as the forces of history gathered around her and the men who were so eager to be her partners. Eventually Joe Altemus, a draftsman, caught her eye, partly because he was good-looking and partly because he had a "cute" Ford convertible. Even more than dancing, Grace discovered she loved talking with Joe—and no travel or orchestra was required. They talked for hours and then hours more. When Joe was sent away to Basic Training, letters replaced talking, and they wrote so very many letters. He returned to Bethlehem Steel afterward, trim and tanned, but with one specific mission in mind.

"He walked into the office," Grace told anyone asking about those days, even long after she was happily remarried. "We were engaged that night. He told me he always knew." In another email to John, her long-buried emotions pressed even closer to the surface, like the shrapnel that for years resided in my father's leg. "Joe and I really belonged—that's the best way to describe how I felt about him." With a brush of remarkable candor, she ends the passage, "I had better stop."

For anyone who has experienced the loss of a loved one, it isn't hard to understand the strong emotions that made Grace's retyping of Ray's June 1945 letter painful. Indeed, Ray himself says the letter was hard to write. It was his very personal memory of the crew's last mission and final moments, at the time of the writing more than a year in the past. Joe Altemus's role in Ray's story must have made the hearing of it all the more difficult for Joe's grieving young widow.

Ray's letter set the stage for the crew's final flight. "After briefing at the Intelligence Office, usually George [Goddard], Kandy [Kandarian], Spick [Spickard] and Joe arrived at the plane together," Ray wrote, "but that morning Joe was by himself. That eagerness and happy smile were not there (that was the first real thing I noticed). Because I always liked to kid him about the target, that morning I just couldn't say anything. About ten minutes later, Joe told us the target was Regensburg, the farthest point ever hit in Germany by the 15th Air Force."

Before the crew had a chance to start grumbling, or even succumbing to fears of what lay ahead, Goddard called all of them together and uttered what virtually became his epitaph. "Boys, it's Regensburg, and you can expect the worst."

In trying to help Grace and the families he knew would read his words understand, Ray went to considerable length to take us into the too-real world of a superstitious bomber crew. He mentions that Mel Adams was taken sick that morning, so Staff Sgt. Oscar Houser was ordered to take his place as engineer. "Never flown without him," Ray said of Adams. And there was another first contained within their mission: Miss Fortune would be flying tail, going in "last and low." Ray must have depicted the formation somehow, for Grace was able to peck it out on her typewriter for the families, using clusters of x's.

Last & Low Group 22,000 ft.		First & Middle Group 22,500 ft.	Second & High Group 23,000 ft.
	X 1st element	X	X
	X X	X X	X X
is	X 2nd. element	X	X
	X X	X X	X X
	X	X	X

Miss Fortune, like other B-24s heading to Regensburg, carried ten 500-pound bombs. The bomber left the ground in Italy at 8 a.m., with the bomb run projected for about 1 p.m. It was only when they reached fifteen thousand feet that Ray noticed Dusty Rhodes, who "stared in a corner with a twinkle in his eyes and white as a sheet." Ray realized it was Rhodes's last required mission. After this, air combat would end for him. If, Ray began to consider darkly, there was an "after this."

Ray's letter takes the reader for a look into the cockpit as the plane nears the Alps and the weather turns bad. He asserts that the crew always trusted Goddard to do them right in the pilot's seat and also respected Kandarian as co-pilot, mostly for being "pleased to sit up and sweat it out" beside the man he seconded. The temperature, Ray says, reached 40 or 45 degrees below zero as the Alps rose up below them, slicing huge chunks out of their distance from the ground and offering no flat or welcoming place to set down in an emergency. The crew already knew the drill: By the time they'd dropped their bombs and started back to Italy, the mountains would be littered with burning B-24s as though they were campfires. Miss Fortune hit the "turning point," the spot for "go or no go," and flew on, even as other bombers in the group developed mechanical problems and headed for home. "This we did not like," observes Ray, "because we were losing firing power." Again, Ray and Grace provided useful diagram of the Alpine crossing.

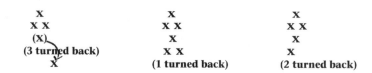

As they left the mountains and focused on reaching Regensburg, the cannons firing flak far below started belching, and the oily black splotches started to fill the air around them, in front, behind, on all sides, the force of the explosions shaking Miss Fortune as its men prepared for what they knew was coming. Ray in particular knew, having been there on December 19 when a shell from a German fighter devastated my father. As this day's fighters began to swarm, choosing their angle of attack, Ray skidded away from his waist gun just long enough to warn his mates—he specifically mentions John's uncle Wayne Nelson—to keep their eyes open. On the very first attack, Ray watched as the wing of a B-24 flying nearby tore off between its first and second engines. "I watched it go down till it disappeared out of sight," Ray reports, his written tone factual, without emotion. "Saw no one bail out." And from that moment on, there was little the crew of Miss Fortune could do except fight for their lives.

"Bombs away," shouted Spickard, an announcement that at least promised the plane could start turning toward home. Firing his own .50-caliber at fighters as they rose, twisted and dived, Ray listened in terror as ball turret man Harold Carter announced that his .50-calibers had frozen up. Goddard told him to do anything to get them working, and then one of the guns started firing again. Nelson was firing away, reloading as quickly as he could. It was then that Ray thought he smelled something through his oxygen mask, perhaps the worst thing a flyer in his position could smell. Ray ripped off his mask and struggled to gaze down into the bomb bay, now relieved of its ten five-hundred-pounders, and he hated what he saw. The German fighters still circled, some passing within feet, and the flak still exploded all around them. The plane shook from wind and close concussion, as well as from Goddard's attempts at evasion. But the thing that made Ray catch his breath was the sight of what he'd smelled: fuel flowing in rivers into the plane's bomb bay.

Looking out through Miss Fortune's open waist gunner positions, Ray Noury realized that the plane, which had lifted off from Italy hours earlier with so much strength in numbers, was absolutely and terrifyingly alone.

In addition to sharing Ray's details of that horrific day, Grace's correspondence with John Torrison began to create a relationship between the two of them. His reference to feeling an echo of his parents' Florida home when visiting Grace and Buddy was no accident, as email after email between them makes clear. When she was not reminiscing or talking about her challenges with the computer (opening attached photos seemed especially difficult), she wrote about the latest doctor and hospital visits for herself, her husband or both. In the chatty style of another era, she talked also of two of her sons, who lived for a time in Hawaii, lamenting that neither was married and therefore she had no immediate prospect of grandchildren. She even kept John posted on her efforts to find a missing dog, a beloved family pet named Scooby.

Grace's long marriage to Buddy, in dramatic contrast to her short marriage to Joe, also emerged in her correspondence with John. Buddy had been career military, serving with Gen. George S. Patton's Third Army as it raced across Europe in the waning days of the war. Buddy had retired from the military and gone to work at Kennedy Space Center; their residence in Cocoa Beach was not far from the launch pads of Cape Canaveral. Her deep love for Buddy—and what might have been her deep love for Joe, had he lived—shone through in her detailed, caring and never self-pitying accounts of the aging man's serious medical problems. It was a vignette of love and fidelity surely being enacted across America by those who'd fought and survived the Second World War.

The search for details of Joe's death had faded over the years—marriage and children in the present tense supplanted the past. Yet with age came memories, and with memories came a certain profound curiosity. That must have been what kicked in when Grace was perusing her husband's retired officer's magazine and saw that Joe's old unit was staging a reunion. There seemed little reason for her to attend, of course, and indeed in one of her emails she expresses concern about how her current husband might interpret this interest. Buddy assured Grace he had no problem with her tracking down as much as she could about her first husband.

The magazine article led her to 98th Bomb Group historian Herb Harper, and he pointed her in two directions at the same time. One was to Ray Noury, whom she remembered well from his June 1945 letter. Yet when she spoke with Ray on the phone, she felt she was intruding more than anything else and that he didn't want to talk about this anymore. As John discovered in speaking with Ray, and I discovered later, nothing could be further than the truth. Her suspicions seemed to reflect her own inner reluctance, especially as members of the World War II generation passed away, to engage children and grandchildren in memories that had little meaning for them and were, for anyone who truly cared, heartbreaking. Grace's initial belief that Ray didn't feel like revisiting February 22, 1944, was reinforced when she eventually phoned Skipper Goddard. In both cases, however, Grace eventually developed warm relationships built on a link that had remained dormant for six decades.

As best I can tell from the emails, Grace's efforts to follow Herb Harper's lead to what was now being called the Czech Republic progressed fitfully. Along the way, she unemotionally reports on commemorations in Nepomuk and its surrounding villages, itemizing her series of returned letters and unanswered emails to the people behind them, questioning Harper repeatedly about whether she was using the correct address.

At one point, things started looking up: Grace received a letter from a young Czech man who said he'd found Joe's dog tags and the wreckage of the plane on the hillside back in 1991. Because the country had been under communist rule from 1948 until 1989, nothing officially had been done to excavate the crash site or to memorialize the crew. All that changed with the fall of the Iron Curtain, explained the young man, who said he was now writing a book on the subject. He included photos of dog tags, a monument and a recent dedication ceremony. He also asked Grace to send him a photo of the crew for his use in a collection of artifacts that were turning into a museum, which Grace agreed to do. The young Czech man also mentioned that, as World War II entered its final days, the remains of the crew had been taken to France for burial. Grace wrote back to him but never received a reply.

All this activity, especially with John's research efforts enriching Grace's personal memories, attracted media attention. While admitting that most of her life's media connection came from writing a local shopping column for *Florida Today* for a year or two, she does seem pleased that a reporter named Billy Cox came to her home to interview her in 2004. Running on Memorial Day, the piece headlined "WWII widow finds closure: Letters written 60 years ago help family heal" tells the story in the clipped style of daily journalism. It tells the story of Grace's life, weaves in the contributions of Ray Noury and the significance of John's research, culminating in his first trip to Nepomuk with Ray.

"It's a wonderful story, and Grace was very pivotal," John told the reporter. "My mother's dead now, and all of Wayne's siblings are gone. Why that one letter of Grace's was saved, I don't know. I know this has been really difficult for her. But her spirit, and the way she's been able to carry on her life with an enduring love, is one of the qualities we all aspire to."

In early June 2004, Grace found herself fascinated by the TV coverage of D-Day's sixtieth anniversary, the Normandy invasion that launched the final Allied assault on Fortress Europe—fascinated enough to email John about it. Regardless of whether Grace understood the strategic connection, D-Day was the top-secret plan behind Big Week, which sent Miss Fortune deep into Nazi Germany. In all the talk of brave men scrambling up bloody beaches on June 6, and fighting through the hedgerows of France in the days and weeks that followed, no one talked about the Eighth and Fifteenth Air Force bombers that destroyed German aircraft manufacturing capacity in the months before D-Day to remove the threat of air attacks on invading Allied troops. Yet an anniversary that would mean even more to Grace was still almost a year away.

It was late April 1945, and Patton's Third Army was on the move. In the last offensive of the European War, the now-five hundred thousand men of the Third massed along the Czech-German-Austrian border. As was his style, Patton wanted to push ahead. He had his eyes on Prague, he told Supreme Allied Commander Dwight Eisenhower and General Omar Bradley, and he wanted to get there and claim the grand old Czech capital before the Red Army could.

The complicated situation was quickly becoming more so, Patton was told. The Soviets were Allies, not merely America's next enemy, and the decisions being made about life in Europe after Nazi Germany were political, not military. At last Bradley called again, telling his aging friend the warrior, "The green light is on for the attack of Czechoslovakia." How soon can you go? "Tomorrow morning," Patton responded with his signature bravado.

The response from one German outpost in these final days was entirely different from the response from the next—one group fighting to the death and another surrendering with considerable relief. Even the local population showed differing reactions to the victors. Nazi sympathizers among the villagers were abject and belligerent, while as the troops drew near Plzen, the red, white and blue of Czech flags started to appear in windows all over town. In Plzen, citizens lined the streets ten deep. One GI described the scene ecstatically: "It was Paris all over again."

Patton's Third Army liberated village after village, town after town, pressing onward in the direction of Prague but all too aware of where they had been ordered to stop. The army moved more slowly now, stymied not only by orders but also by eighty thousand Germans who wanted to surrender.

In one Czech village Patton's troops liberated, there was an additional report: an American B-24 bomber had crashed there more than a year earlier. The villagers had gathered and buried the crew's remains nearby in a single, shared grave.

CREW PHOTOGRAPH TAKEN ON FEBRUARY 15, 1944. TOP ROW L TO R: GEORGE GODDARD, HAIG KANDARIAN, CHARLES SPICKARD, JOE ALTEMUS. BOTTOM ROW L TO R: RAY NOURY, WAYNE NELSON, HAROLD CARTER, MEL ADAMS, ROY HUGHES.

CHAPTER FIVE
BATTLE STATIONS

I left Houston before dawn one Saturday in March 2014 and drove to Austin-Bergstrom International Airport. Thanks to a gift from my wife, Maria, I was able to rise into the chill Texas Hill Country air aboard one of two B-24 Liberators still flying in the United States. I climbed in through the open bomb bay doors, poked around the interior while on the ground, and then hung on as the pilot opened up the throttles. The ancient bomber shuddered, the propellers disappeared in a blur and we ambled down the runway. I glimpsed a Southwest Airlines 737 waiting to take off behind us and thought about how sturdy it looked compared to the aeronautical senior citizen in which I was seated next to the rear bulkhead. Once aloft, I felt the steady throb of four 1200-horsepower Pratt & Whitney engines and heard the roar of wind inches outside the waist gunner's position, where I naturally gravitated.

This plane carried no bombs. No mountain ranges lay ahead, no fighters lurked above, no batteries of flak surrounded Bastrop in the fields below. I still found myself wishing, as I imagine those flying aboard Miss Fortune did, that the plane's structure was stronger, its aluminum thicker.

Considering the B-24's suprising fragility, the courage of those who manned its battle stations seems greater still. As I moved and looked about, each of those young faces from all those grainy, blurry black and white photographs rose up before me. I saw them at work that February 22, each doing what he considered his job, stocking up on shaky confidence against the death that waited for them just beyond the thin metal skin.

My desire to know more centered on my father's story. I was generally aware that others had flown with him, but these other crew members initially were cast in my mind as supporting players in the story I wanted to explore. Conversations with Ray, John Torrison and Grace quickly realigned my thinking. I began to realize that each crew member had a family sweating out the missions back home. Each took off from Italy as a young man with the unrealized promise of a life ahead. I eventually understood that no one crew member is more central to the story than any other. The only important distinction is the one between crew members who got to live their post-war lives, and those who did not.

GEORGE GODDARD

GEORGE GODDARD
Pilot

"Even though I never knew my father," Skipper Goddard Miller wrote to John Torrison, "I always felt a strong connection to him through my grandparents. I learned much about him when I traveled to Texas to spend summers with them in his hometown of Ennis. My father grew up in this small town atmosphere, where everybody knew everybody and everyone knew George. There were pictures of him everywhere, and I thought he was very handsome indeed."

George Goddard was attending what then was called North Texas State Teachers College in hopes of becoming a school teacher when war broke out in Europe and the Pacific. Like many of his generation, he was convinced the Axis powers were a threat to human freedom, perhaps even to human existence, and good, basic, everyday people had to do everything in their power to stop them. It was a simple, unnuanced belief, but these were simpler, less nuanced times. George practically ran to the recruiting office and signed up to become a pilot in the Army Air Corps. He was only twenty.

By the time he turned twenty-three, Goddard was piloting B-24s over Europe, devoting himself to the air war that was helping to tighten the noose around Hitler's Germany. The mission in the air had evolved, especially as the Allied powers knew that Big Week was approaching: from protecting troops on the ground by out-flying and outshooting their Luftwaffe fighter counterparts to destroying the factories that kept them in the air. Cities like Augsburg and finally Regensburg became an undesired part of George's geographic vocabulary.

Before he set off on what proved to be his final mission, George received exciting news that his wife was expecting a baby. As his crew aboard Miss Fortune had already taken to calling him "Skipper," the naming flowed naturally from there. "Little Skipper" the child would be, both to the crew for its brief time remaining and for the rest of Skipper's life.

The training pilots received to fly the B-24 seems short: a nine-week course followed by 120 hours of flying time earned the pilot's gold bars. A further two months were typically spent learning the B-24 specifically, along with the nine or ten men assigned to it. According to pilots of the day, knowing the men, their habits, strengths and weaknesses, was essential. When the plane was in combat mode—fighting for its life—there would be no time to figure anything out. The B-24 pilot was the pilot second; first and foremost, he was the airplane's commander. He led men into battle, just as if he were at the head of an infantry or tank unit.

There was one additional challenge facing Goddard and his fellow B-24 pilots—nearly every mission strategy in the book was configured for the more numerous B-17s, what the world came to call the Flying Fortress. There were many technical differences between the two aircraft, not the least of which was the B-24's faster optimum cruising speed. Yet the planes often took off and flew together to the same target. As a result, to keep the group from separating, the B-24s frequently were relegated to the rear of the formation, where they soaked up the punishment whenever the Luftwaffe attacked. Out there on their own, Lt. Goddard had learned first-hand more than once, they were vulnerable.

HAIG KANDARIAN

HAIG KANDARIAN
Copilot
Haig Kandarian from Fresno, California, had more reasons than most to fight for America. His parents, Ruth Enochian and Levon Kandarian, had come to this country from the region known as Armenia— though its status as a recognized nation would remain disputed. They escaped in 1910 from the portion of Armenia that belonged to Turkey, just as the long-denied Turkish genocide of Armenian people was beginning. As writer William Saroyan has chronicled, for many Armenians living in the city or the vast agricultural areas around Fresno, America became a sacred place of sanctuary.

Haig grew up around two older sisters, Agnes and Leona. All three of the Kandarian kids graduated from high school, and Haig managed to squeeze in a single year of college before the coming of war made his higher calling obvious. By 1940, Leona was the owner of a grocery store with a soda fountain across the street from the high school. I picture young Haig spending hours there, nursing the last from a chocolate milk shake or a banana split with pals who knew their friend's big sister was in charge. There would come a time when virtually no young men would be around to sit at that soda fountain.

Haig Kandarian must have seen what was closing in on this country a bit before most Americans. Though the between-wars isolationism trumpeted by Charles Lindbergh and others of lesser fame remained popular, Haig enlisted in the Army Air Corps on October 2, 1941, a full two months before Pearl Harbor changed a lot of people's minds about America's safety in the world. The day before Miss Fortune took off from Italy on its bombing mission to Regensburg, Haig Kandarian turned twenty-one.

The relationship between the copilot and his pilot could be strained by pecking order tensions, but Kandarian always got along well with Goddard. Kandarian was second in command of the unit, and therefore responsible for everything Goddard was—although he remained a step beneath Goddard in authority. He had the same training essentially but perhaps fewer hours of flight time when he got the call to join the crew. Because of this pecking order, pilots fresh out of training almost never volunteered to be copilots. It was something they were assigned. Once in place, however, sitting beside the man in charge in the B-24's cockpit, Haig and any other copilot earning his pay knew there'd come a time, sooner rather than later, when rank mattered far less than survival.

CHARLES SPICKARD
Bombardier

CHARLES SPICKARD

One of Charles Spickard's distant grandfathers served as a foot soldier in the Revolutionary War that followed America's Declaration of Independence from Great Britain and eventually joined the new country's main army under General George Washington. I have seen no mention of what "Spick"—as the crew invariably called him—thought about this fact from history, but I wonder whether it gave him courage for the battle ahead.

Charles was born in 1921 to Charles and Lou Belle (Tinsley) Spickard in Kansas City, Missouri, though by the time he was twelve or thirteen his parents had separated and his mother had remarried. We don't know any details about his stepfather, Russell H. Forquer, except that the marital turn of events made Charles a lonely young man. A family friend later recalled to John Torrison: "Charles (Pinky to us) didn't have any family other than his mother Lou Belle. There were no brothers and sisters. Pinky spent most of his time with my dad and our family, and was considered family. After Lou Belle married, I understand he pretty much moved in until he graduated high school."

Trying to find his place without a true father in a world of boys who had one wasn't easy, but Charles did show enthusiasm and aptitude in baseball and the Westport High School auto club. Once he'd graduated, he worked as a clerk in a local paint store while he attended college for one year. He enlisted in the Army Air Corps in 1942, finishing his training as a bombardier in Midland, Texas. Years later, Ray Noury would described his buddy Spick as "a guy who attains results. Worked hard at his job, always hitting the target with accuracy."

Spickard's training placed him within a large and often feisty group, not least because many in bombardier school had recently failed to make the cut in pilot training. Such guys were itching to show off, to outdo the pilots who were flying the plane, occasionally even to make them look bad—as though to demonstrate that they could have handled the pilot's job better after all. No fewer than forty-five thousand bombardiers completed the 20-week training during the duration of World War II.

Though most considered their training sufficient, especially when it came to using the Norden Model M bombsight and eventually the much-better Sperry S-Series for accuracy, there was no way to gain precision through practice. In the bomber group flying out of England, for instance, so many bombs fell on empty fields instead of targets that a wag re-christened it the "8th Agricultural Air Force." For Spickard and his fellow bombardiers, this was not emblematic of poor work but of too many unknowns, including poor visibility due to cloud cover or flak, very high altitude, pressure from German fighters and wind. By February 22, 1944, the Air Corps accuracy reports were getting better with each passing day.

JOSEPH F. ALTEMUS
Navigator
Joe Altemus's marriage to Grace Malloy created the bond that had ignited the surviving families' search for information. By sharing Ray Noury's letter with the crew family members she could locate, she created an extended family joined in grief as the military's barometer moved inexorably from "missing in action" to "presumed dead" through 1944. Without Grace's love for Joe, the families

might not have had a story to tell—or the strength to remember it.

At his birth in 1916, Joe became the fourth of seven boys. It was natural that he would go to work at Bethlehem Steel, since it was the town's primary employer. Other businesses, from the pharmacy to the café to the bank, tended to support and draw from the main one. And in this man's world, requiring the strong backs and thick arms that had helped America become steel supplier to the world, Joe worked as a draftsman until the day he met Grace.

JOE ALTEMUS

On March 10, 1943, soon after that meeting, Joe enlisted in the Army Air Corps, and not much later he left for training in Cuba. By then, the two were close enough that they would write each other each day they were apart, and secure enough in their relationship that Joe could simply ask Grace to join him at Langley Field in Virginia so they could be married on August 30, 1943. The wedding took place only a month before he joined Miss Fortune's crew and headed overseas.

As with bombardier and several other jobs on B-24s, navigation school tended to attract men who had not been successful in pilot school. There is, however, no evidence that this was Joe Altemus's path. A bit older than most of his crewmates, he was apparently drawn to the 20-week course for its own sake, landing there only after a mandatory six weeks of gunnery school. Navigators often took over the nose turret position; and they needed to be fast and accurate with a .50-caliber for the survival of the plane.

Trainees like Joe spent 104 hours in the air before being assigned to a unit, probably working aboard Beechcraft AT-7s to master the compass and a wild collection of hopelessly interwoven variables like wind drift and air speed. As technology made leaps forward under the pressure of war, other skills became important too. Navigating by radio bearings came along to supplement traditional sight navigation with the help of charts, as did newly developed techniques for flying at night.

A commission as a second lieutenant and a pair of silver wings awaited those who completed navigation school. In the case of newlywed Joe Altemus, so did a navigator's job aboard a B-24 bomber headed for Italy.

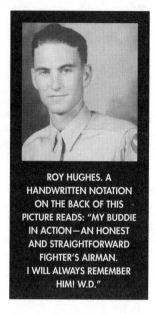

ROY HUGHES. A HANDWRITTEN NOTATION ON THE BACK OF THIS PICTURE READS: "MY BUDDIE IN ACTION—AN HONEST AND STRAIGHTFORWARD FIGHTER'S AIRMAN. I WILL ALWAYS REMEMBER HIM! W.D."

ROY HUGHES
Radar/Top Gunner

Among the memorabilia left after my father's death, I found a formal military portrait of Roy Hughes, who handled radio and radar duties aboard Miss Fortune and who, under enemy attack, took the top turret position. Scribbled on the back I read: "My buddie in action—an honest and straightforward fighter's airman. I will always remember him! W.D."

Roy Elton Hughes grew to manhood in northern Texas during that region's grinding Dust Bowl years when it was all a farmer could do to scrape up enough produce or money to put a few bites in front of each family member once a day. It may have been no accident that Hughes turned out to be rail-thin. Born in 1921, Roy and his family settled in the town of Friona by the time disturbing reports started coming in from Europe and the Pacific. His father, Buford Hughes, worked at a car agency, and Roy rose into some of the same universe by pumping gas at the local station. His mother, Lucy Mae, stayed home to take care of her son and his four sisters.

According to his mates aboard Miss Fortune, Roy was the best gunner they'd ever seen, cool and quiet in his deadly work, as contrasted with others who became overexcited when lives were on the line and made fatal mistakes. He was, the crew members said, always efficient. Apart from work, he was well liked for talking, always showing up with a smile and, as Roy Noury expressed it later, loving his family "with all his heart." Perhaps this love, much appreciated back home in Friona, was the inspiration of the words on Buford's grave marker: "He gave his only son so others may live free."

The crew had every reason to respect Roy's efficiency; as jobs on a B-24 went, he had one of the most complex. It fell to Roy to service, maintain and operate all communication electronics on the plane, which included both radio and radar, plus tuning units, the radio compass, frequency meters, the telegraph key, transmitters and receivers, even the emergency flare supplies and Verey pistol for use if the plane went down. The radio man usually sat on a backless stool above the rear portion of the bomb bay, hunched over a small metal table that held the receiver on top and the transmitter underneath. The position was uncomfortable, a fact that became an issue on long runs like the run to Regensburg.

The cold realities of combat flight meant that each radio man was also trained as a top turret gunner, a nose turret gunner and even a waist gunner. Among other skills, Roy Hughes was virtually the only man on Miss Fortune with training to fix the gun turrets if they jammed in the heat of battle.

WAYNE NELSON
Tail Gunner

John Torrison's uncle Wayne, known as "Lord Nelson" to his Miss Fortune crew mates, was a third-generation Norwegian-American in a part of the country that must have seemed a suburb of Scandinavia at times. Most of his great-grandparents migrated to America from the Valdres Valley in Norway around 1860 and settled in a farm town with an only slightly different name—Valders, Wisconsin.

With three brothers and four sisters, Wayne was the family's youngest child. Baptized and confirmed at Our Savior's Lutheran Church, he is now honored with a beautifully engraved B-24 gravestone in the cemetery of that very church. Sadly, Wayne's mother never did quite accept

WAYNE NELSON

MEMORIAL TO WAYNE NELSON IN VALDERS, WISCONSIN, WHICH WAS UNVEILED IN 2004.

that his plane had crashed, that he was not in an undiscovered POW camp or that he was never coming home to Valders again.

Friends and crew mates consistently described Wayne as quiet, as well as serious about whatever studies he undertook. He was apparently quite literate and literary, known both for loving to read and for keeping up a steady stream of letters to his brothers and sisters. The portrait that emerges is one of a calm young man who seldom went out, except when he simply wanted to relax with the guys he flew with, and who never had a harsh word for anybody. Ray Noury admitted that he liked Wayne so much because he wanted to be like him. "The best pal a fellow would ever want," Ray said.

In the parlance of the war, the tail gunner was the man on each B-24 "who looked steadily at the past." This "steadily" was not entirely true, for the position did not encourage takeoffs or landing in the swiveling turret that poked out the back of the plane. It was considered close to lethal to try it, since the forces involved could whip the gunner's head against the gun sight. The turret, therefore, was where Wayne climbed each time Miss Fortune was safely and smoothly airborne. He climbed back out each time Miss Fortune drew near to its landing strip.

The tail gunner's clear Plexiglas and armored glass turret, like all of its swiveling kin aboard Miss Fortune, resembled nothing as much as a Christmas ornament with machine guns poking out of it. Riding in the turret was cramped and, high above Europe, teeth-chatteringly cold. Its terrific visibility made the position vulnerable to being the first place shot up by a German fighter or the first place shattered by exploding flak. One tail gunner remembered reporting for his first day of duty, being shown to his plane—and then being told that a maintenance crew was busy vacuuming the remains of his predecessor out of the turret that would be his.

RAY NOURY
Right Waist Gunner

It's unclear whether Ray Noury understood he was volunteering for the coldest place to fight aboard a B-24. Still, his upbringing in New England, rather than in Miami or Los Angeles, may have at least taught him to be resistant to the cold. Ray joined the Army Air

Corps before Pearl Harbor made the Axis powers suddenly up close and personal to most Americans, when there was no guarantee the United States would ever enter the war. His initial plan was to get in and get some training, then transfer to the Royal Canadian Air Force, which was connected to Great Britain and therefore already in the fight for survival.

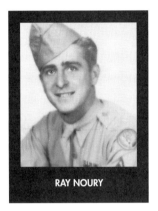

RAY NOURY

In the beginning of his service, warm weather was the norm. With the Japanese attacks in the Pacific having ushered in a cruel new reality, Ray was first sent on anti-submarine patrols aboard Douglas DB-7s before heading for Havana. It was there, in the bright Caribbean sunshine, that crews of B-24s were being pulled together. Fighting planes like Miss Fortune were essentially born as units in Havana. And then the sun followed Ray and the rest to North Africa. When the base became liberated Italy and the mission became Nazi Germany, the weather changed abruptly.

Nothing comes through more clearly in the memories of waist gunners than the cold. They fired their .50-calibers out a large and utterly open window, with winds roaring in at 170 or more miles per hour and temperatures worthy of the Arctic. Frostbite among waist gunners was not uncommon, even when they were wearing the electrically heated "blue bunny" suits. Icy temperatures were cited as both blessing and curse by men wounded in the position, some complaining that their skin was frozen so hard that no one could force a needle full of morphine to penetrate and others reporting that a limb spurting warm blood failed to kill them because the blood froze to make a seal.

There was one upside to the waist gunner's unpleasant and precarious position. In addition to the large windows for firing on both right and left sides of the plane, there was a floor hatch that gave waist gunners a better chance of escaping when the plane started to falter. Ray's position aboard Miss Fortune was perhaps the only one from which he might have fallen out as he did, miraculously waking on the solid ground fifteen thousand feet below.

With deep roots in French Canada and his local French Canadian community, Ray was fluent in French. At the war's end, however, he turned down a job as an Army translator and embarked upon life as a civilian. He married, raised six children and, for a time, owned a grocery store near his hometown in Rhode Island. When, in 2002, Ray the sole survivor accepted a Distinguished Flying Cross, he was adamant how and why he was willing to take the medal. "I can accept this honor, not on my behalf, but rather on behalf of my crew."

JOHN GOLDBACH

JOHN A. GOLDBACH
Left Waist Gunner

It is intriguing to ponder the "substitutionary death," the death that came about in battle because someone was in a position that, had things been different, would have surely been filled otherwise. Had my father not been seriously wounded on December 19, he by all odds would have been the left waist gunner on Miss Fortune on February 22—which means he probably would have perished that day with every crew member except Ray Noury, and I would never have been born. Instead, it was John Goldbach.

Known as "Goldy" to his crewmates, John was born in 1921 in Lehighton, Pennsylvania. Both his father, Edward Francis, and his mother, Emily Pauline, were born into families that emigrated from Germany, in this case during the 1880s. The jobs these families took reflected their roots, and John's father worked as a meat cutter. With six sisters and two brothers, John lived long enough to see two sisters find jobs as tailors in a local shirt factory. John loved sports and worked in a grocery store after finishing high school; he never had the chance to consider further education. He met his wife, Ida Sweeney, while he was working at the grocery store.

John enlisted in April 1942, getting trained as a gunner in North Carolina before heading overseas. He and Ida were married in the summer of 1943 while John was home on leave. She never remarried after his death.

There are indications he flew missions with the 330th Bomb Squadron before finding a station with Lt. Goddard's B-24 while my father fought for his life on various operating tables between Italy and Ohio.

Ray called his friend Goldy "a fighter if there ever was one," a remarkable flourish of knowing praise. Ray would have seen what the man was made of, because in battle, they fought off Luftwaffe attacks virtually back to back. The definition of courage as "grace under pressure" seems to have applied to Goldy. At St. Peter and Paul Catholic Church in Lehighton, there is a marker in the cemetery where family members are buried. The marker describes Goldbach as "T/SGT US Air Force Lost in Action WWII."

REXFORD RHODES
Nose gunner

A survivor of the famous raid on Ploesti, Romania, Rexford Rhodes was almost finished with his war. He already had a Distinguished Flying Cross to prove it.

Realizing that the enemy required fuel not only for its planes in the air but also for its tanks and troop transports on the ground, the Allies set their sights on the oilfield surrounding Ploesti. There were at least two noteworthy attempts to destroy the oilfield, the first on June 11, 1942, involving thirteen B-24 Liberators. An oil depot was seriously damaged, as was the port of Constanta, from which much of the oil was shipped. Perhaps most dramatically, this Ploesti raid was the first by the Allies against a European target.

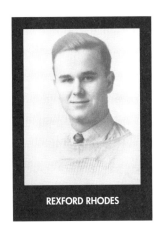

REXFORD RHODES

The second and larger raid, in which Rexford Rhodes won his DFC, sent no fewer than one-hundred seventy-seven Liberators from bases in the Libyan desert to Ploesti in August 1943. The damage was significant, but the casualties were staggering. The planes dropped some three hundred tons of bombs from smokestack level, producing horrific memories of flying through the flame and smoke created by their efforts. Fifty-four B-24s were lost in that raid, and three more crashed into the sea. Operation Tidal Wave, as the raid was called, produced five Medal of Honor winners. Three of the five medals were awarded posthumously. With losses like these, it is little wonder that replacement B-24 crews, like the one assembled around George Goddard in late 1943, were needed so urgently.

Rhodes flew on Miss Fortune in February 1944 to complete the number of missions required to go home. He had, in Ray Noury's memorable words, already "gone through the mills."

All on board Miss Fortune believed that February 22 would be Rhodes's final mission. In such cases, whenever good sense could be applied, the goal was to assign such guys to "milk runs," short and relatively easy meanders over as safe a target as possible. The anxiety that all on Miss Fortune felt when they heard the word "Regensburg" not only came from self-preservation. It also had a lot to do with Rhodes's final flight with the Army Air Corps being the deepest trip over Germany that the Fifteenth Air Force had yet attempted. With the superstition virtually all flyers felt and Ploesti on his resume, Rhodes must have wondered if he was seriously pressing his luck. As a result of his last-minute assignment, there are no photographs showing him with Lt. Goddard's crew.

REXFORD RHODES RECEIVES THE DISTINGUISHED FLYING CROSS FROM GENERAL DOOLITTLE IN OCTOBER 1943 AFTER THE RAID ON PLOESTI, ROMANIA.

Born in 1919 in New Lisbon, Missouri, Rexford grew up as the son of Dallison Rhodes and the former Ida May Harwell. By the time he turned twenty, he was living in Poplar Bluff and listing an uncle on his mother's side, Dr. James Harwell, as his guardian. Rexford worked as a night clerk in that town's Gibbons Hotel before enlisting in the Air Corps at Jefferson Barracks in January 1941. Rexford's military service proved to be all about the B-24, since he was assigned to Northern Star flying missions out of North

Africa as the Allies focused their efforts of Hitler's Germany. One history-making result of that focus was the daring raid on Ploesti.

HAROLD C. CARTER
Ball Turret Gunner
Moving around was no oddity for American families during the 1920s and 1930s, especially as the employment rigors of the Great Depression took hold. For Harold's parents, Cleburne and Rheathelma Carter, however, holding a job was less effort than following one around. Cleburne worked to build bridges all over Ilinois, taking his family with him each time he got a new assignment. Harold Cleburne Carter was born in 1922, finally settling in the small town of Carlinville, Illinois by 1940.

Like most of Miss Fortune's crew, Harold had a host of siblings: four brothers and two sisters. They all called him Cleburne, his middle name given in honor of his father. The young man finished high school and took a waiter's job in a local restaurant before enlisting in the Army Air Corps in October 1942.

He was assigned to Goddard's crew before leaving the States, then enjoyed a brief, pub-filled stopover in Ireland on the way to combat in North Africa with Ray Noury, my father, Roy Hughes, Mel Adams and Wayne Nelson. A photo captures the visit, the six uniformed guys wearing expressions ranging from muted smiles to

CREW MEMBERS POSE FOR A PHOTOGRAPH IN AN IRISH PUB ON THEIR WAY TO ITALY IN LATE 1943. L TO R: RAY NOURY, BILL BOYCE, ROY HUGHES, MEL ADAMS, HAROLD CARTER, WAYNE NELSON.

emotionless at a dark table. In battle shortly thereafter, Ray decided that Harold "always put his heart and soul into everything he did."

The swiveling ball turret that could be cranked down from the belly of a B-24 was known as a "Death Trap." For Harold C. Carter and the rest of the men who climbed into the ball turret, the name proved chillingly apt. Within a short time after Miss Fortune's fateful attack on Regensburg, B-24 crew after B-24 crew lobbied commanders to remove the ball entirely. For all sorts of technical reasons, the amount of good a ball turret gunner like Carter could do paled in comparison to the cost in weight and danger.

Technically speaking, the Briggs/Sperry retractable ball turret was one of the air war's most fascinating developments, essentially giving each B-24 "eyes" on its underside to cover what otherwise would have been a blind spot. It did what it was supposed to do. Because it required the ball turret gunner to climb into it before it was cranked down below the plane by the waist gunner, it did the crews far less good than its inventors had hoped. It was nearly impossible to escape from if the plane got into trouble, since no one was free to crank it back in. One of Ray Noury's final memories before falling out of Miss Fortune on February 22, 1944, was struggling to crank Harold Carter back into the plane. As Ray would write in his letter to Grace Altemus: "Tried to bring it up hydraulically but no success."

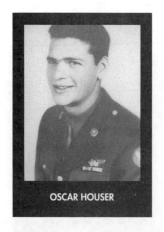

OSCAR HOUSER

OSCAR W. HOUSER
Engineer

When a B-24 was hours from home over enemy territory, with the snow-peaked Alps or a vast ocean in between, it was impossible to call a repairman when something stopped functioning. That's why nearly ever bomber crew took off, and hopefully landed, with its own engineer. Part of getting Miss Fortune back to the place where it could land safely was the job of Oscar Houser.

Born in Philadelphia in September 1920, Oscar was the son of Edward and Verna Houser Yeakley. He had two older brothers and one younger sister. Verna was only nineteen when he was born, a fact that may or may not have had something to do with what passed for his childhood. For parts of the 1930s, Oscar's older brothers went off to live with their grandparents in Ohio. It was during this presumably difficult period that he decided to use not his father's but his mother's surname. By 1940, with war on the horizon, he was Oscar Houser—even as Verna was marrying August Clements and starting to go by his last name.

Oscar attended three years of high school in Philadelphia but abandoned schooling to work cutting soap in a local factory. He enlisted in the Army Air Corps in August 1941, only months before the attack on Pearl Harbor. Ray Noury considered Oscar to have a "strong mind and kind heart," but he alluded to a deeper sadness when he said the man "had a tough time but fought to the end."

After the war, one B-24 commander praised the typical engineer for "his wide knowledge of the airplane," and observed that "flying the B-24 becomes miserable work if you have a weak engineer." As with other key positions, a lot of the men who ended up engineers had initially trained to be pilots but had not succeeded in that program for one reason or another. By official assignment, the engineer was not qualified to fly a B-24 by himself, though some were forced into doing so; he was, however, qualified to take over as a bomber's co-pilot. There were added things in the job description that hint at an all-round knowledge of the aircraft: parachute non-commissioned officer, first-aid specialist, assistant radio operator and leader of the crew's enlisted men.

These open-ended duties kept flight engineers like Oscar Houser busy throughout most missions. They didn't have to wait for Luftwaffe fighters to attack in order to go to work. One of their most crucial tasks, in fact, happened before each and every flight, when they climbed and crawled all over the aircraft, externally and internally. If the aircraft received a clean bill of health, engineers were expected to poke their heads out a hatch at the top of the fuselage during the taxi along the runway, on the lookout for planes and other obstructions.

The same ritual took place when the plane landed on the ground at the end of each mission: the engineer's head poked out through the open hatch, his mouth and nostrils sucking in the breeze. He knew that he and his buddies had survived one more mission, one more day.

As I learned about the crew's history, I was struck by the mixture of backgrounds. My father, a streetwise and restless teenager from Washington D.C., put his life in the hands of sons from small town Texas; the children of immigrants from Armenia and French Canada; a smart young guy from a tough Pennsylvania steel town; the descendant of a Revolutionary War solider; a refugee from the Depression who rode out tough times in southern Illinois; and a sturdy kid from Wisconsin farming country. And they put their lives in his. Later in my research, I got an inkling of how my father felt about being separated from his crew. I'm not sure he ever fully forgave himself for surviving. If he was tough on others at times, he was that much tougher on himself.

HAIG KANDARIAN'S MOTHER RUTH, HIS SISTER LEONA, AND HAIG.

CHAPTER SIX

TWO KANDYS
FROM FRESNO

Mary Hevener of Walnut Creek, California, never met Haig Kandarian. Indeed, she never heard of him until 1972, when her father married a woman named Leona, or Lee, who became her stepmother.

Leona proved to be an extremely private person, remaining something of an enigma through the final seven years of Mary's father's life. In fact, few even knew her by the name her parents gave her or by its shortened form she used in bright, chatty letters to her brother Haig, whether he was in Army Air Corps training in the United States or co-piloting a bomber based in Italy to bring down Hitler's empire. Everyone knew her as "Kandy," which had been her brother's nickname until the day Miss Fortune fell from the sky.

As Leona passed ninety, because of her failing health, Mary became her trustee and custodian, eventually moving her stepmother into an environment where she could get the care she needed. Taking on this role, she essentially became the trustee and custodian of something else as well.

"While going through her possessions at her home after she moved," Mary says, "I found a lot of memorabilia about her brother Haig. I knew he died during the war, but the only thing Kandy told us was that he was a wonderful brother and it was very sad, and especially hard on their father Leo. I never knew there was a survivor, or that they were buried and remembered after all these years."

At first glance, there isn't much to Haig's effects saved by his sister and now treasured by his sister's stepdaughter he didn't live to know. A couple of newspaper articles over the years sketch in brief pieces of the family's history, including the arrival of Leo and Ruth Enochian in the United States in the early 1900s, refugees from atrocities committed against Armenians by the Turks. Like so many Armenians, they settled in Fresno, California, and set themselves to the difficult but rewarding work of produce farming. And as is common to many ethnic groups who found shelter in the United States, they felt an immense loyalty and love for the country that had rescued them from the storm.

From the moment Mary Hevener took possession of all that apparently remained of Haig's Kandarian's love for family and country—a couple of high school-style yearbooks from his aviation training, some casual on- and off-duty photos, some bound logs of his training flights and then real ones ending in the flak-filled skies over Nazi Germany, and a smattering of letters from Leona to her brother—she felt they should mean something to somebody. Somebody, she believed, perhaps a World War II archive somewhere, should place a value on these things, since that would place value on the lives of the people they represented. But she discovered no one who did. "Reading the letters, seeing the pictures tugged at my heart," Mary says. "I was told, 'No one wants those things. There's a lot of that stuff out there.' So I tucked them away, never thinking I would someday get a letter from John Torrison."

When John tracked Mary down as part of his research into the crew's history, the materials Mary had protected began to make sense. They took on a context, a storyline. Long-empty blanks that Mary had recognized, struggled with and surrendered to for decades were filled. Along the way, Mary had contacted two living first cousins on Leona's mother's side, Bob and Gloria Enochian.

Bob didn't remember much about Haig—"it was a long time ago." She even found a half-written letter her stepmother penned to a historian in 1984, after he had contacted her about relatives who'd lost their lives in World War II. As best Mary could tell, the letter was not finished and definitely never mailed.

Most of all, in a way sadly similar to my relationship with my father, Mary could never ask—was never allowed to ask—her stepmother about all she knew of her brother. General questions about the family made it through the filter sometimes, including the two families' escape to America, but moving toward Haig proved to be moving toward something dangerous. Even questions about what to do with his effects (along with his father's little desk, an Armenian Bible, family pictures and his mother's dish) met only a wish to "think about it later." It simply hurt Leona too much to talk about the brother whose nickname she still carried. To Mary, holding onto this name seemed a kind of slightly secret tribute on Leona's part. "She maintained/maintains her privacy to this day," Mary wrote.

Mary allowed John and me to review a few hundred pages of Haig's military records, related documents and correspondence. Although Leona could not talk about her brother, a trove of official Army Air Corps records does a good bit of the talking for her. These documents detail Haig's training in various parts of Texas and Virginia leading to the trip overseas from which he'd never return. The top sheet for February 1944 on the right side of the folder concludes with the date February 22, the aircraft type B-24J and the result (Missing in Action).

Mary also provided two framed photographs of Haig and a selection of smaller snapshots. Haig was clearly a handsome man, the kind the girls of his day would have gone for even without his superior co-pilot's pay, generous enough for him to be able to take them out for dinner and even dancing. At the time of his death Haig sported a thin, Errol Flynn-style mustache, and in photos he looks like some combination of Tony Curtis and Sal Mineo in their movie star primes. In one framed shot, Haig is merely walking toward the camera away from a cluster of long buildings that formed some kind of military base, a lone stack rising in the distance and emitting curls of black smoke. Haig looks happy enough to be there, wherever there is—but not nearly as happy as in a second framed photograph.

In this one, he sits with a pretty girl and another flyer at a table in a café or cafeteria, the two men with menus, their now-mystery date curiously without. Perhaps they were in the habit of ordering for whichever young lady had caught their eye. To the taste of the early 1940s, while the other two people look attractive, Haig could be a model, ready to tout cigarettes, after-shave or the latest model of Chevrolet.

In a selection of unframed photos, there is a single photo of an older man. The photo credit reads: "US Army Air Forces, Hamilton Field, California," meaning that the photo was taken not far from the family home in Fresno, perhaps during one of Haig's leaves or other excursions to his home state. The man has Armenian features, though without the very traditional bushy mustache; his suit is well-pressed, and his necktie hangs from a light-colored dress shirt. He doesn't yet look traumatized, since after all he was surely at Hamilton to visit with his son. There is, however, a certain sadness in his eyes.

The rest of the shots supplied by Mary Hevener are military, including a dashing one of Haig behind the controls of a plane. Since co-pilots were trained to be pilots, he is pictured in the main seat, with only the blurry suggestion of dials and gauges around his view outside through the glass. Other pictures range from staid and posed—groups of Haig with two or three buddies standing at attention—to a series of shots showing some of the same guys during and after rifle practice. A final image shows Haig perched atop a stone piece of fence with what appear to be pine trees stretching off toward the horizon. He wears the faintest of smiles. Most of all, from photo to photo, the future copilot Haig Kandarian looks very thin and very young.

Mary's collection includes two overlapping variations on Haig's pilot's log from his training days: a small blue spiral-bound number with each flight carefully noted in pencil, complete with date, time of takeoff and landing, and perhaps most important to a pilot in training, number of minutes in the air. Logging a specific number of hours flying is what the training program is all about. In the notebook, there are scratches and extra notes from time to time, quite unlike in the official leather bound logbook published by Air Associates Inc. The log itself is full of rules and warnings for pilots and students about keeping an accurate (and mandatory) record "of their flying time and the nature of their flight," including any accidents. "All entries," the book declares with finality, "must be made in ink."

Each flight Haig made, beginning May 2, 1942, was carefully written across a two-page spread, noting the type of aircraft (PT 19-A Fairchild at the start), the make of its engine (Ranger) and whether the flight qualified as "local" or "cross country." Not surprisingly, all Haig's flights until June 22 were listed as local. According to the log certified correct by the sergeant in charge at Kelly Field, Texas, later in Haig's training, he would fly planes by Vultee and Beechcraft as well.

Haig's effects include three thin yearbooks. They resemble those published each year by high schools, except they are devoted to the young men in training to be Army Air Corps pilots and the men who taught them. Haig's class, known as 42-J, dedicates its edition to those who've trained and taught them, "sincerely hoping that we may be able to repay a small portion of what has been given us by helping our country in its battle to continue as a free democratic place in which to live." As in high school, especially nearing the end of senior year, classmates wrote in the books. The most touching comment in Haig's copy (noting his nickname beneath his portrait as "Kandy") comes from a fellow known as Twin Pistol Ball. "Haig old boy," the fellow student pilot writes in blue fountain pen, "Be careful and be sanitary, because we'll both try to hedge hop our graves when they start to put us in them. To the best pal in the business the best of luck, and I'll see you in advanced or in Burma."

One of the clearest pictures in Mary's collection of Haig Kandarian's time and place comes from a letter written by a close friend named Wally Barr. Somehow it ended up among Haig's things at the house in Fresno and was gathered with his wartime memorabilia after his death. The letter was typewritten with more spirit than grammar on

May 10, 1941, addressed "Dear Drunkard" and mailed from Wally's air base in Albuquerque, New Mexico, to Haig's family home on M Street in Fresno. Echoing a conversation going on across the nation in the months before America entered the war, Wally encourages his friend to join the U.S. Army Air Corps rather than sign up in Canada in hopes of getting into the fight a bit sooner. "Don't be a dam fool," he writes. The presumption is that America will enter the war, with only the "when" a bit of a mystery. The "why" for enlisting was certainly no mystery. "They will be needing lots of men," Wally writes of the U.S. Army Air Corps, "and it would be better to fight for your own country than another, don't you think? After all it is the best country in the world."

Wally also updates Haig on his adventures with the opposite sex. He has, as of the writing, met "a swell girl named Ruth—she is twenty-three and has been married and has a little girl three years old and has her own apartment and we had a nice party there last night." Telling Haig of his new love interest inspires him to make sure his friend knows he's not dating Janet anymore. The reasons for the breakup, for all the timely vocabulary, seem timeless. "I told her I was going to get a motorcycle and she wrote me and said that I could choose her or the motor, well I ain't about to let any woman tell me what to do so I took the motor." But then he adds, "I think I'll wait till I get home to get one as I can get credit there easier."

The two-sided folder of Haig's military records provides the best understanding of his service after he enlisted. Each sheet was clipped in atop all previous sheets until the one noting "(Missing in Action)." Beginning May 2, 1942, much of his basic flight training took place in Texas, initially at a base near Brady in the central part of the state. By fall, Haig trained with missions out of Langley Field in Virginia focused on formation, night flying and instrument flying, and by early 1943 he ran anti-submarine missons out of the Army air base in Jacksonville, Florida. By this point, he was no longer flying small, single-engine trainers; Haig had moved up to dual-engine B-34s as he moved from "aviation student" to "pilot."

Things took a darker turn on September 28, 1943, when Haig was transferred from Langley to APO #12441-AH, NYC, NY. The record doesn't tell where he actually was, since such information—taken together with thousands of other bits—might tell an enemy where troops are being concentrated and therefore what the Allied strategy might be.

The monthly pages list six missions aboard a B-24 in October, with Haig as co-pilot to different pilots in all of them; he served for a few hours here and there as "day pilot" in two of them. November was slower, with only three missions but then his schedule picked up the following month. In the final month of 1943, Haig flew fourteen missions, with him logging time as "day pilot" on ten of those. Presumably these were longer flights, including the bombing mission to Augsburg on which my father was seriously injured. That would be covered in the day's sortie report, but not in the direct, emotionless chronicle, without so much as the name of a place, that forms the record of Haig's service in the air. January was, again, a little slower, as we now know the Army Air Corps was gathering its forces and finalizing its strategies for Big Week. February 1944 brought eight new missions, culminating for Miss Fortune on the 22nd.

Of the seven letters Mary possesses written by her stepmother to her brother overseas, five are particularly heartbreaking. While one was written before Miss Fortune crashed into that hillside near Nepomuk, all five letters were returned to the sender. Each is signed across the front of the envelope "William B. Sawyer, Major, Air Corps" beneath the single forlorn word: "Missing."

The final letter from Leona, dated March 15, 1944, stops far short of desperation from not hearing back, but concern creeps into her voice as she writes about her efforts to have Hershey send chocolates to the crew. "We are all anxious to hear from you again saying that you have received our first package and what kind of condition it was in when it did get to you," Leona writes. And later, "Everything here at home is fine but all waiting for the day when you will be back with us again."

HAIG KANDARIAN'S FATHER, LEVON, RECEIVING HAIG'S MEDAL.

Haig had been dead for twenty-one days.

A touching letter penned in late November 1943 is intriguing as the earliest appearance of Grace Altemus in the Kandarian circle. It is also the last extant letter from Leona to Haig that he lived to read.

"Today we received a card from Grace Joe's wife," she writes from Oakland, "telling us she had heard from Joe saying that Spick, Joe and you were together and that you all were enjoying a cup of tea at the club." To close the same paragraph, Leona expresses a single, simple wish, starting with hearing from her brother as often as he can write and suddenly moving on from there. "To know just some of the small things you are doing makes us feel that you are so much nearer," writes his sister, signing as "Lee." "Hope you are all fine and that you won't ever have to be separated from each other."

Mary sent one packet of materials to Houston, and then another. She found more letters, postcards and telegrams—180 of them—not from Haig's sister but written by Haig himself to her. It was exactly the entry point into the lives, and voices, of Miss Fortune's crew that, frankly, I wish we had for every single one of them. Mary's years of preservation, when nobody else had use for these materials, suddenly felt more crucial than ever.

Reading through Haig's letters from earliest to last (postmarked by the Army February 22, 1944, no less), I realized that nothing much had to happen to inspire communication. Today, we might even ask: Why? It dawned on me that the real reason these letters were written was to connect, to break the cycle of distance and isolation that wartime forces upon families. A summary of Haig's letters, taken together, might be: Hope everyone is fine, why don't you write more often, I'm sending money when I can, please send chocolate and cake, they keep me awfully busy, I'm here with a great bunch of guys, and I gotta go now so I'll write more next time.

The impact of this voice from beyond the grave is extraordinary, the mundane nature of Haig's day-to-day life before he started flying crucial bombing missions over Europe making his rare flourishes of eloquence or profundity all the more heart-wrenching to read seventy years after his death.

The earliest letter in the collection is dated October 7, 1941, and heads to Fresno from "Private Haig Kandarian" in San Pedro, Calif. It describes experiences that any young person might note in a first letter from the service. "The camp sure seems quite [sic]," Haig writes. "Everything here is sure clean and neat (when I say neat and clean I mean that we can't have a wrinkle on our beds and not a speck of dust or dirt anywhere in the barracks or kitchen)." Home still seems close and eternal in this letter penned before the Japanese attack on Pearl Harbor pressed the United States into war. "Say hello to Bill and the rest and tell them to write. Tell me how you are making out at the store and etc."

By Haig's letter home of October 20, he had joined Flight #9 of the 26th School Squadron at Jefferson Barracks outside St. Louis. This letter particularly affected me because by the time I read this letter, I knew that Jefferson Barracks was the place that, after two burials in different parts of Europe, the mixed remains of Haig and the other nine men of Miss Fortune would at last find a permanent home. This letter has a printed P.S. added by a friend named Dave Lutton to Haig's often-hurried but legible script: "Just a line to inform you that Haig and I are two of the roughest, toughest, cussinest, straight-shootinest, tobacco-chewingest, K-pinest, high-falutnest, hard-workenest yard birds that was ever cussed out by a sarge."

THE CREW'S GRAVE MARKER AT JEFFERSON BARRACKS NATIONAL CEMETERY.

As 1941 became 1942, the updates home came from a series of different camps and military schools as Haig slowly pursued his growing dream of becoming an Army Air Corps pilot. That meant understanding planes—virtually any kind of plane—and knowing how to fix whatever might break, especially when lives were at stake in combat.

As I read through this new trove of letters, details that were missing from the sparsely worded records I had seen before filled in a much more intimate picture of his experience. The letters are postmarked Denver (where Haig writes from Lowry Field, "Please for my sake do not worry, because I am in good hands and in the branch of the army which is highest respected and more taken care of") and then from a host of locations in all parts of Texas. These begin with Harlingen where the Gulf meets the Rio Grande Valley and continue through San Antonio ("We start school tomorrow and have ground training here for five weeks"), Brady and Sherman.

Further corroborating the monthly pages, letters from other courses Haig took came from Jacksonville, Florida and Langley, Virginia, and he sent his family a single postcard from Havana, Cuba. By this point, some of the chattiness disappeared from Haig's voice, apparently the result of growing certainty of a posting to the combat zone mixed with wartime censorship. "Not allowed to say much," he wrote. "Will write when I get back. Learning a lot of Spanish here. No one knows how to speak English."

A new theme found its way into Haig's letters from wherever he was stationed by 1943: his family clearly worried about him in light of bad news from the European war. American soldiers were dying in battle—boys they knew from families they knew. In letter after letter, Haig carefully tried to calm their very understandable fears for his safety.

"Please don't worry about me like that anymore," he wrote from one flight school with almost-painful transparency, "because nothing will ever happen to me I'll see to that myself. If I get through this course you will have something to be proud about and so will I." In another letter, Haig wrote with unexpected urgency, "I'm sorry of little but it is of great importance. I sure miss you folks but when this war is over mark my words I'll be over to see you +

and my predictions are always right. I always wanted it this way so I am considering myself lucky. I am with the swellest fellas + and the best squadron in the Air Force." And finally, within days of the lieutenant's departure for Italy in late 1943, he wrote: "This may be my last letter for a long time... I'll be a captain when I get back mark my word. When you get my clothes have them cleaned and pressed because I'll need them when I come back... Most of all I want you to do me a big favor + and that is to not worry, because I told you I am coming back + I mean it."

On February 16, 1944, Haig envisions a family reunion, some-day and somehow, once the victory has been won—and once his communication won't have to make it past the censors. "Tell Dad when I return I am going to sit down by him for a month straight and tell him the most interesting stories he has ever heard that he can't see in the news reels. And when I return he and I are going out and have the biggest celebration he has ever seen. Ask him if that is a date." A couple lines later: "We'll have the biggest meal you've seen. Just our family."

On February 20, two days before his death, Haig sent his sisters a delicate handkerchief he bought during a quick trip to Sicily and promised to send the two others he'd purchased in upcoming letters. After years of signing his letters home "Haig," he signs this one with an affectionate, brotherly "Bud." The handkerchief shows a white dove flying through flowers and offers simply "Ricordo della Sicilia." Not postmarked until February 22, the letter was probably the last thing Haig Kandarian ever wrote.

HAIG KANDARIAN SENT THIS HANDKERCHIEF FROM SICILY AS A GIFT TO HIS SISTERS ON FEBRUARY 20, 1944.

I looked at Haig's handkerchief and pondered how luck was dis-tributed at twenty-five thousand feet above Germany. The airmen's luck was their families' luck, too. My father had luck—of a sort. So did Ray. They bought tickets home at a steep price paid in install-ments for a lifetime. Haig and the others never returned to families who were no less deserving of post-war lives with their husbands, fathers, sons and brothers. Rexford Rhodes may have had the worst luck of all, beating the brutal odds over Ploesti only to die on his last required mission. As far as luck goes, Miss Fortune was good to me. I knew my father, received his love, rode out the storms, and watched him build a productive life. Miss Fortune denied that opportunity to George Goddard's daughter. And Leona Kandarian was left to mourn her handsome brother's memory for decades in a place beyond the reach of words.

THE OFFICIAL ARMY AIR FORCE'S CAPTION ON THIS PHOTO READS AS FOLLOWS:
"FATHER MISSING IN ACTION—CAPT. HERBERT R. DAILEY, ADJUTANT AT FIFTH FERRYING GROUP,
PINS AIR MEDAL ON TINY DRESS OF VANCIL RUTH, DAUGHTER OF LT. GEORGE M. GODDARD OF ENNIS,
MISSING PILOT. MRS. GODDARD HOLDS BABY, NEVER SEEN BY FATHER."

CHAPTER SEVEN
LITTLE SKIPPER

T he most powerful image of Skipper Miller is an official photograph showing her receiving a medal for valor on behalf of her father. Skipper—or "Little Skipper," as Miss Fortune's crew referred to her—is in her mother's arms. She is less than one year old.

I first saw the photo when I flew to Jacksonville, Florida to meet Skipper during the summer of 2014. According to the official Army Air Force caption, the photo shows Captain Herbert R. Dailey pinning Lt. George Goddard's Air Medal on the dress of his infant daughter, Vancil Ruth Goddard. The caption says: "Mrs. Goddard holds baby, never seen by father."

The picture was a punch in the gut. I could not decide which image punched hardest—the face of an uncomprehending and fatherless Skipper, who looks directly into the camera, or the face of her mother. Evelyn Goddard is not looking at the camera, and she is not looking at Captain Dailey. She looks off into the distance, her jaw set in grim determination as she endures a ceremony that no wife or mother ever would envision for herself. This picture depicts the hole left by a thunderous impact—taken from a different perspective, but just as distinct, as the crash-scene photos snapped by Czech villagers on a cold February day in 1944 and now on display in Nepomuk.

In the comfortable home she shares with her husband Jack, a retired engineer, Skipper seemed to harbor no bitterness about the events that made her the "crew baby," the only child ever born to the men who perished on Dubec Hill near Nepomuk. She exhibited more pride than sadness concerning the father who died overseas before she could ever see him or let him hold her, before she could reach out and touch his mouth, his nose, his ears. Skipper Miller has lived a long life since the death of George Goddard, helped along by the fact that her mother Evelyn remarried and gifted her with a stepfather who also loved her. Most importantly, Skipper learned to love her real father from the man and woman who loved him first.

"When I was little, I'd spend most of every summer with my grandparents in Ennis, Texas," she recalled, naming the then-small town about thirty miles south of Dallas. "They'd dress me up like we were heading to church on Sunday and take me around to the bank, the hardware store, everywhere they needed to go. And I remember everybody called me 'George's daughter.' They'd introduce me that way, whenever we met anyone on the street. 'That's George's daughter,' they'd say. I was being shown off, and people made a big 'do' over me. And I could tell everybody in that town was very proud of my father. 'We loved your Daddy,' they'd tell me. And I grew up thinking he was a very special person. He was a hero in their eyes."

George Goddard spent his entire childhood in and around Ennis. He'd been a star of the Ennis High School football team, even returning to give a speech after graduation on the benefits of athletics—the script of which Skipper showed to me during our visit. He earned his senior ring from EHS and wore it proudly into combat in the skies over Nazi Germany.

Like most who've come to value their relationship to Miss Fortune's crew, Skipper forged a friendship with Ray Noury late in his life. She and Jack visited Ray and John Torrison in Boston as part of a vacation trip to Kennebunkport, the seaside resort village in Maine. "We sat there talking about the crew and, well, about everything for three or four hours," she remembered. "They had to kick us out of that dining room." As time passed, Ray got in the habit of phoning Skipper each Memorial Day and each February 22, while she got in the habit of phoning him each Christmas—until 2013. "His daughter answered. When I asked if I could speak with Ray, she said, 'Oh I guess you don't know. My father passed away about a week ago.'" Ray had been her last human link to George.

SKIPPER GODDARD MILLER AND RAY NOURY IN 2004.

"I love talking about my Dad," she said to me, leafing through pages and photos of memories in a plastic storage bin, "even though I never knew him."

George, the passionate pilot who couldn't wait to start flying missions against the enemy, met Skipper's mother Evelyn in an airport. She was a ticket agent for an airline, Skipper recalled, and that day George was flying somewhere as a passenger. The two hit it off, got in touch and, with the expedited emotional schedule wartime brought on, were soon married on May 23, 1943.

There was little or nothing by way of honeymoon, and new-lywed life was tied closely to the frenzied training attached to going overseas. On the day George's plane took off for Europe and its destiny, Evelyn was carrying George's child. The news was cheered by every member of the crew. They unofficially named the child-to-be—referring to it often as "he," as even Evelyn did in her letters—Little Skipper, or sometimes in a sentence "The Little Skipper." The men were proud of their Skipper. They knew George would do everything in his power to fulfill each bombing mission and get them all home safe. They knew the baby boy coming soon would be worthy of his father's legacy.

The yellowed photo of Skipper receiving her father's medal shows her mother looking movie-star glamorous; it's easy to understand how she took George's heart when she was only supposed to take his plane ticket. "You know," Skipper said, looking up from the picture with a smile, "people ask me why I still go by my nickname Skipper after all these years. And certainly, I thought more than once about using my real name." She paused with perfect comic timing. "But really, my real name is Vancil. How much of an improvement was that going to be?"

Skipper was an infant and toddler through much of the worst, especially that first year of not really knowing. Her memories of that time are limited, and based more on what she was told than what she experienced at the time. Her mother remarried some three years after her father's death, happily for Skipper, encouraging the child to stay close to her grandparents in Ennis. Her grandfather was actually a conductor on a train, so that meant she could travel from Jacksonville to New Orleans (with her mother early on, but later by herself), meet her grandfather there and travel onward to Ennis. Sometimes she could stay only a week or two, other times most of the summer.

She may have basked in her father's still-fresh memory during those slow, simmering months, filled with the pleasures of any Texas small town, but she also was happy at her home the rest of the year. Her mother had chosen a good father as well as a good husband. The man adopted Skipper to make it official, always treating her with the love he would have given his own child.

Skipper grew up, got married and had two sons (and now three grandchildren) of her own, often thinking back as a grandmother to the affection and acceptance George's parents had shown her in Ennis. After all, they might not have. They might have spent the rest of their years buried in grief and bitterness over the son the war took from them, as most assuredly some parents did. Even more likely, her mother might have seen her "new life" with a new husband as requiring her to cut all ties with her past. This she did not, even if it meant keeping George alive in a way that surely was more painful than not. She did it for Skipper, because she thought it was important. And, she did it out of love and respect for him.

Skipper's grandparents in Ennis passed away, as did her own mother and stepfather—George Goddard's memory moving with finality into that plastic storage bin. Then, one day in 1993, the phone rang.

"Is this Skipper Goddard?" the unfamiliar voice asked. "I've been trying to find you."

The caller was a "Colonel Oates" from Ennis, who had known George Goddard growing up and was aware of his death in World War II. Lt. Colonel Oates was positioned near the end of an unlikely string of people who had set out to find her, beginning at Miss Fortune's crash site in the Czech Republic.

When Miss Fortune crashed on February 22, 1944, people rushed up Dubec Hill from Nepomuk and surrounding villages to look at the wreckage and take pictures. The crash was a big event in local history; the memory survived among residents of the surrounding villages despite Nazi occupation and the later arrival of the communist regime in what was then Czechoslovakia. Local residents remembered where the crash site was and occasionally dug around it to uncover artifacts; they did so despite the risks during the communist era, when showing any curiosity about the American contribution to the Soviet Union's "Great War" was forbidden.

One of the curious local residents was Vaclav Majkut, who risked arrest to dig around the site several times under the communists. After 1989's Velvet Revolution, when forty-one years of official communist rule ended after hundreds of thousands of protestors took to the streets in Czechoslovakia, Vaclav and his son Rene had freedom to excavate the crash site without fear of arrest. In 1992, Rene presented his father with an intriguing find from the crash site: a ring recovered from the mix of mud and dead leaves bearing the initials "GMG."

Vaclav heard about a man in the area named Manuel van Eyck, who was asking questions about the B-24 crash on Dubec Hill.

Only fate, it seems, could have connected this father and son in this tiny village in the Czech Republic to a colorful (and colorfully named) figure like van Eyck. Officially listed as hailing from "North Hollywood," van Eyck was a writer and researcher with a particular interest in American planes lost over Eastern Europe during the war. This was not entirely surprising, because he was born in Czechoslovakia in 1947, escaped into West Germany in 1969 and, upon arriving in the United States the following year, volunteered and served in Vietnam.

Based on his own research into United States military records and local Czech history surrounding the crash, van Eyck had learned the names and home towns of the B-24 crew members who died on Dubec Hill near Nepomuk. After Vaclav Majkut met van Eyck in 1992 to discuss the ring Majkut's son had found, van Eyck concluded that "GMG" stood for "George Marvin Goddard" of Ennis, Texas. Majkut and van Eyck decided that they would attempt to find a relative of Goddard's who would appreciate having it.

GEORGE GODDARD'S ENNIS HIGH SCHOOL CLASS RING.

In February 1993, van Eyck wrote to the chief of police in Ennis and asked him to locate any living relatives of George Goddard and offer them the ring, perhaps by showing the photo around town or placing a "small article in local papers which are read in your region." If that quest failed, van Eyck had one additional suggestion: "Perhaps you could find cemetery where parents of Goddard are buried and insert this ring into their grave. I think they would approve it."

The Ennis police chief promptly called Lt. Colonel Oates, who had gone to high school with George Goddard in Ennis. Oates tracked down Skipper in Kansas City, Kansas, where she was living with her husband Jack under her married name, "Miller."

"I felt goosebumps," Skipper remembers of the 1993 phone call from Oates that ultimately led to the return of George's class ring to her. "It was like a ghost had walked into the room."

And the ghosts were not finished with her.

John Torrison also had been searching for Skipper. He learned her married name and located her in March 2004. After an exchange of letters, John visited Skipper in May 2004 and brought Ray with him. Ray gave Skipper a batch of letters. Although there were no letters from George Goddard in the collection, it did contain a window into Skipper's own first year on this earth. The letters were written by her mother and mailed from Jacksonville to Central Falls, Rhode Island, addressed to either Mrs. Marie J. Noury or, in the more traditional style, Mrs. Joseph Noury. They went north from "Mrs. George M. Goddard Jr." when George was still missing in action, when there was still every reason to keep hoping for his return. There were three additional letters at the end, written by Evelyn to Ray when he had made it back from the POW camps in 1945, barely a month after Germany's surrender. "Know you've heard 'it must be wonderful being home again' so much," Evelyn writes on June 13, 1945, "so I'll just say I'm very happy and grateful that you are home among your friends and family again."

The earliest letter in the packet Ray shared with Skipper, and presumably the earliest letter he had from Evelyn to his mother, is dated April 3, 1944, just over a month after Miss Fortune's crew was declared missing in action. In the opening, Evelyn introduces herself, even though she says she suspects their names have been used together in earlier communications from the Army or other family members. By the third paragraph, she is ready to deliver one of the simplest and best summations of the thousands of letters about "our boys" that must have crisscrossed America throughout the war.

"I do hope you feel as we all do, that they are safe and well, wherever they are," Evelyn writes. "I just know that they are alright and if everyone will keep the right thoughts, they will be back soon. I feel sure that we'll hear good news soon. There are so many ways of their getting through by means of the wonderful Underground Systems over there, or they could be in Switzerland, or Prisoners of Germany. Oh, we have so much to hope for." In this initial letter she addresses Ray's mother as "Mrs. Noury." As the letters flew back and forth between them her addresses become endearments—"Dearest Mrs. Noury" and eventually "Mom Noury."

By the time Evelyn wrote again on April 19, 1944, word had arrived that Ray was a prisoner of war, and while she conceded that this was "not the best thing," she insisted that it gave her hope that all the other crew members were safe as well. They may not be all together, she said—all the crew families seemed to fixate on the boys being together, wherever and however they were—perhaps they were somewhere in twos and threes. Evelyn asked Mrs. Noury for the address at which she could write to Ray via the Red Cross and she presumably wrote to him there—but no such letters survived to be in the packet. "I know that George," she wrote, "would want us to keep in touch with him and the rest of the boys and their families." Before she closed, there were two other quick notes: Evelyn has located and written to "Sgt. Boyce," and she regrets not being able to go visit him in the hospital because she is expecting a baby in about six weeks. "Maybe Raymond mentioned it to you as the boys all called it their 'crew baby.' We've nicknamed it 'Skipper,' and I just hope and pray that I'll know where George is when the time comes."

Taken together, Evelyn's letter from May 26, 1944, and an apparent, undated reply from Mrs. Noury demonstrate the amount of information, conjecture and wishful thinking moving between the families of missing airmen throughout those months. Letters often contained references to other letters.

In her typed letter of June 14, 1944, (nearly all the others were handwritten), Evelyn recounts for Mrs. Noury a rather long and involved story about hearing of an airman from a Texas town fifty miles from Ennis—Cleburne—who'd just made it home after being declared missing in action. Lt. J.C. McClure was actually part of the same Regensburg mission as Miss Fortune and had seen George Goddard's plane in formation in several raids, even though he was based twenty miles away and did not know the crew personally. This McClure connection was so promising that George's mother first called him for information and, since he was reluctant to talk on the phone, went to see him in Cleburne.

McClure, a bombardier who had been shot down three times, provided what likely was the crew families' only description of the Regensburg mission before Grace Altemus circulated Ray's

"Our Last Mission" letter in June 1945. The day was "very cold" and there was a "2,000 ft. undercast" that made it difficult to spot the targets. In the course of his conversation with Mrs. Goddard, McClure mentioned all the accepted truths of that time—that there was an active and generous underground that rescued and protected downed American flyers, that there were standing instructions to head for Switzerland if your plane got into trouble (even though news of a crew's survival would be slower from Switzerland than if they were captured by the Germans), and that the overall odds were excellent. "Lt. McClure said that the people in America will be surprised to know how many of our boys will turn up after this war that have been missing or killed in action," Evelyn reassures herself more than anyone else. "He said there would be thousands."

In the envelope with this typed letter is a smaller envelope, this one containing a pink-rimmed card from "Lt. and Mrs. George M. Goddard, Jr.," announcing the birth of Vancil Ruth Goddard on June 3, 1944. The baby girl—the Little Skipper—weighed eight pounds, four ounces when she arrived.

Letters over the months that followed are full of baby news, not surprisingly—including one from Evelyn about receiving her husband's personal belongings from the Army. "Among them is a little baby bib he had bought when he was in Sicily. It had a picture of a little boy on it. Won't he be surprised when he finds that the Skipper is a little girl?" That year's Christmas card from "Evelyn, George and Skipper" was mailed from George's hometown of Ennis, where Evelyn and the baby were visiting. By December 26, 1944, Evelyn wrote that she had moved in with her mother in Dallas, keeping house to help her while she worked. After asking about Mrs. Noury's Christmas, Evelyn offered the simplest report imaginable. "I guess all of us crew families had a quiet one this year."

The final brief letter to Mrs. Noury from Skipper's mother comes in May 1945. By June, when she first wrote to Ray, he was home in Rhode Island, the war in Europe was over and—most distressingly—the crew families have received no joyous news. In her first letter to Ray, Evelyn essentially put him on the spot, insisting he write and tell her everything he knows about the events of February 22. The news might be "dreadful," she said, but it will be better than the "suspense." By her second letter, Ray has written his letter to Grace Altemus and she has retyped it and sent it to all the crew families. They have read it and understood it as what it almost certainly was: an unofficial obituary.

"Someday," Evelyn wrote to Ray of his letter, "when Skipper is old enough, I'll give it to her. I just hope I can do justice to all of you when I explain to her about her Daddy and his swell crew… I'm so grateful to you and the rest of our gallant crew. I know that they didn't die in vain and because of them and others like them little girls and boys like Skipper will have a safe and peaceful world to live in. I pray that God will give me wisdom in raising her, so that she will have nothing but love and kindness in her heart for everyone. I'm going on as I know George would want me to. I'm going to try to live up to his bravery and courage, because though I long for him humanly, I'll always be with him in spirit."

When I first saw the December 19, 1943 sortie report, I thought about the crew's courage only in reference to the considerable bravery required to fly into Germany on Miss Fortune. I had to consider further after reading letters from Evelyn Goddard and Grace Altemus. George and Evelyn had been married about four months, and Grace and Joe for about one month, when George's B-24 lifted off from Langley in early October 1943 to carry the crew into Italy and combat. Evelyn was pregnant by then. After June 1945, Evelyn and Grace had to confront the hard truth of widowhood and create new lives for themselves. Their letters betrayed no self-pity. The tone in Evelyn's writing matched the steely look in her eyes as Captain Dailey pinned George's Air Medal on Skipper's dress. She celebrated Ray's survival. She did not complain about the unfairness of her own difficult and unasked-for mission. Neither did Grace. Like their husbands, Evelyn and Grace simply did the impossibly hard task assigned to them. There was no other choice.

Doing the impossible without complaint is admirable; so is consciously choosing the challenging path. The post-war lives and marriages of Evelyn and Grace made me think about my mother's own altered course. Peggy Lesko went to Cleveland in search of news about Harold Carter's fate and met the man to whom she would be married for nearly forty-one years. My mother may have taken on more than she bargained for when she married my father. I am confident it was never more than she could handle. She was a source of unconditional love for me; she also was a guide of sorts who sat at the kitchen table late into the evening and explained how to navigate my father's complicated terrain until I learned to do it myself. Nurse and mother that she was, she knew how to listen. And if she didn't tell me everything, she told me enough to get by when the storms blew in. More than once during the journey launched by my call to Ray Noury, I wanted to sit down with her over a cup of coffee and ask if I was on the right track.

A SMALL BOY STANDS NEXT TO A PORTION OF MISS FORTUNE'S RIGHT WING.

CHAPTER EIGHT

THE EARTH WILL TELL

W hen Vaclav and Rene Majkut were deciding how to return George Goddard's class ring in 1992, Miss Fortune's
crash site on Dubec Hill had been attracting history
buffs and inquisitive townspeople for years. Aging city officials of
the village of Pradlo, the closest significant settlement to Dubec
Hill, insist that public interest in the crash site, and especially in
the men who died there, stretches back at least to the 1960s. That
would place the early stirrings of curiosity well within the confines
of Czechoslovakia's forty-plus year communist period, when curiosity of virtually any kind was officially discouraged.

According to residents who lived through the communist era,
the form of curiosity most disliked by local communist bureaucrats
involved questions about America's role in turning back Nazi aggression. The liberation American troops brought to the beer-lov-
ing city of Plzen and the villages around Nepomuk proved tragi-
cally short-lived. The Nazis had barely departed when the Soviet
Union's Red Army came in. They stayed in one form or another
until the Velvet Revolution.

It is noteworthy, with all these claims of interest by the older generation, that the first two crash-site excavations were carried out not only by amateurs—but by teenagers. The first was Jaromir Kohout. He had heard stories of the crash from the old-timers and had, thanks to an interest in the air war over his native land, found himself fascinated. By Jaromir's logic in 1985, there was only one way to see what was buried up on Dubec Hill—how much had been carted off by the Germans and how much remained—and that was to go there and start digging.

More than a quarter century after his first explorations, Kohout now is the director of a museum devoted to aspects of the air war in Plzen, where he also teaches industrial arts. He was eager in the summer of 2014 to review his diary and explain how his crash-site excavation got started.

"I was eighteen, a student at the technical school where I am now a teacher," said Jaromir, dressed for his day off in a blue T-shirt proclaiming COLORADO: The Mile High State. "My friend from elementary school told me his father was living near Nepomuk. It was his father who told me a plane had been shot down on Dubec Hill. He had been living about five miles away at the time." Jaromir and his brother, Martin, were intrigued by this news. "We wanted to know a series of things, and they became the questions we tried to answer: What day, what type of plane, what nationality and what happened. I was eighteen. I'd never visited any other crash site before."

Despite having no training in such historical inquiries, Jaromir understood intuitively it was important he take excellent, detailed notes of everything he and Martin did at the site, beginning with the fact that they caught the train from Plzen to Nepomuk at 6:51 a.m. on June 29, 1985. This would prove to be the first of dozens of long, descriptive entries covering many trips to Dubec Hill, a series of questions and answers that did not end until May 8, 1992. By that time, Jaromir's interests had broadened to include not only the other two B-24s shot down nearby during the Regensburg mission but an entire collection of air battles in the skies overhead. By that time as well, he knew that another local teenager named Jiri Kolouch also had begun excavating Miss Fortune's crash site.

As recorded in Jaromir's diary, the very first thing he and his brother had to do was deal with the rainwater that always filled the trench dug by the plane's impact. This, he recorded with an eye for minutiae, required 375 bails with a ten-liter bucket, meaning the teenagers had to remove nearly four thousand liters of dark, murky water before they could even start digging. On their first day working the site, they discovered a large steel plate near a piece of the fuselage—still not an answer to the questions. The plate, in fact, was red, a confusing fact in a country still under control of an army and a system that applied red paint to almost anything that could hold it. Still, the suspicion remained that the plane and its crew had been American. It simply made more sense, held up to the narrative told by historians. At some point early on they found a metal plate with a serial number and the announcement MADE IN USA. It was the Kohout brothers' first breakthrough.

"People came around that first day, including an old man who had been a witness," Jaromir recalled. "The gentleman told us the plane had flown from Plzen. 'I heard several explosions in the plane,' he told us. 'It came over the trees and the hills. A wing was missing.'"

Energized by the old man's story, Jaromir and Martin walked the streets of the villages around Dubec Hill, knocking on doors like the police detectives in American movies that no doubt gave them some tricks of the trade. They asked people who looked old enough if they had been there when the plane came down—they still had no date, and they still didn't know if the plane was a B-17 or a B-24 and they still didn't know the astounding tale of Ray Noury. If people said they hadn't been there, hadn't seen anything, Jaromir and Martin asked if they knew anybody who had. In this way, they canvased the entire area for pieces of plane as well as pieces of information. After several visits to Dubec, they'd established enough trust among the villages that people started opening up. And they started digging around their piles of keepsakes for photographs they or perhaps their parents took as crowds gathered around the crash site.

One man had found a propeller, while one woman filled in more visuals of the fatal day from memory. "She told me that after several days the Germans picked up some big parts and carried them off on a truck with a trailer, the kind that carries lumber," Jaromir said. "Someone else told me about a man who discovered a ring. Searching through police records years later, I found that the Gestapo had taken this man to jail."

By July 1986, a full year of visits into the project, villagers had started showing the young men their old photos regularly. One man brought them a photo of a small boy standing in front of the wreckage. "That boy became this man," Jaromir says. "More importantly, I could tell from the flaps behind the boy in the picture that the plane was a B-24, not a B-17." Jaromir made eighty-seven trips to Dubec Hill in all and one two-week foray to the National Archives in Washington, D.C. after the Iron Curtain came down, finally reaching the point he could declare with confidence the crashed plane was a B-24 Liberator.

Talking to everybody who admitted knowing something about the crash turned up the earliest Czech version of the Ray Noury story. It had been set forth, of course, in Ray's June 1945 letter to Grace as well as in Grace's copies mailed to all the crew families. Yet never before, in the country slowly becoming the Czech Republic, had anyone been willing to talk about Ray.

"On June 24, 1990, I met the man who rescued Ray Noury," Jaromir said. "He took me to the place Ray landed. 'It was in the field below my house,' the man said. 'I heard engines having trouble. I tried to locate the plane in the sky, and I saw it over the roofs of houses, the flying plane. I saw an explosion over the woods and a parachute, probably an airman who left the plane in the explosion. The airman landed in the woods, and I ran to him over the field and into the woods. There was snow in the field. I was younger, so for me running was no problem.'"

The man described for Jaromir the bizarre standoff he had with the airman, who was crumpled up beneath his parachute hanging from a tree, "lying on the ground like in need." Ray pulled out a knife when he saw the man approach, ready to defend his life. The man told him, "Boy, I have a knife too, and you might need to put your knife away."

"You German?" the airman asked.

"No, I'm Czech."

Visibly relieved, Ray showed the man he was injured and couldn't walk to safety on his own. The man went to find bandages, then returned and did his best at first aid. Lifting Ray to ride his shoulders, the man started in from the field. At some point, a village woman joined him, helping carry the airman's weight. "Some people said they wouldn't help me," the man recounted for Jaromir. "If the Germans saw me, they'd kill me."

As Jaromir heard the story that day and confirmed key parts in police records later, the villagers took Ray by car to the police station in the nearby town of Blovice, where he was given food and cigarettes. All understood, apparently, that turning Ray over to the local police was the same as handing him to the Nazis. As they explained it to Jaromir, they felt that they had no choice.

"It was not possible for escaping, or any underground," Jaromir explains, shutting the green-covered diary that turned a teenager into a man, a student into a historian researching some of the darkest, most painful days of his homeland. "It was better for an American airman to go to the POW camps."

The second young man to pursue the story, Jiri Kolouch, grew up with a vague but persistent interest in the air war over his native Czech Republic. Jiri, too, had heard the stories about the tragedy on Dubec Hill. Unlike Jaromir, his focus remained on that tiny piece of the war, instead of broadening to take in other B-24s and B-17s shot down by German fighters. Proximity may have had something to do with that, since Dubec Hill figured in Jiri's scenery every day of life. And perhaps his grandmother did too.

"[M]y grandmother was eyewitness," Jiri explained in 2014. "And some people in our village too. So many times I could listen about crash aircraft near village. When we were children very often visited crash site. There was still hollow in ground and some small fragments from aluminum material."

Jiri listened regularly as his grandmother rattled off what had become a kind of collective memory around Pradlo. Around noon on February 22, 1944, people noticed a group of large planes flying over as they were being attacked by Luftwaffe fighters. One was damaged and smoking, eventually losing its wing and quickly going down. There was a "terrible roar of full-running engines followed by a real big and heavy explosion on Dubec Hill. And at the same time an open parachute was seen in the sky."

Jiri was eighteen when he decided with Tomas Tykal and Roman Novak—two friends of similar interest—to follow up on his grandmother's story and find out what happened up on Dubec Hill. The only way to do that was to dig, which they did for three months in 1991.

Jiri was surprised by how much of the plane they were able to find. The pieces they found were stored at Jiri's father's house and became the basis of the exhibit at Nepomuk's museum dedicated some twenty-three years later.

"Logically this event was like magnet to me," Jiri said. "With my friends [I] made the decision to find out what exactly happened here. We had permission from the village aldermen and also from forest administration office. [We] [a]bsolutely didn't know what to expect underground. Some people said: 'There is nothing, German army moved all material away.'"

As with Jaromir's teenaged adventure with his brother Martin, nothing resembling professional excavating equipment was available—not even pumps to remove the ground water that filled and refilled the B-24's crater on Dubec Hill. The teenagers use hand pails to pull out the water, and then hand shovels to see what they could find. Though it was hard work, it was also "really exciting and adventurous," Jiri said. They only money they spent was gas money to go up and down the hill.

The biggest find was three of the four engines from Goddard's plane, discovered approximately ten feet below the surface—"very difficult to get up from mud." With those came other things: propellers, machine guns like the kind Ray Noury fired, ammunition, pieces of the plane's undercarriage and crew oxygen tanks. These things marked breakthroughs for the young men, firing up their long-standing interest in military planes and the act of flying itself. More somber or touching were the personal effects they uncovered. Although their human remains had been collected and buried in a common grave shortly after the crash, the crew's flotsam and jetsam remained. The teenagers found army dog tags, a silver religious medal, cigarette lighters, a sock, a knife—a long-locked window into a moment of human life suddenly opened. A moment that those busy living it didn't realize would be their last until it was too late.

For Jiri, Tomas and Roman, as for John Torrison and me much later, it became impossible to avoid troubling questions about what those final horrific moments must have been like, must have felt like, for the crew. There was invariably the hope that the men were unconscious when those moments came—and a matching fear that they were not.

Today, Jiri's job takes him away from Pradlo on a regular basis, and it has nothing to do with excavating planes shot down over hillsides in long-ago World War II. Many of the people who, like his grandmother, actually witnessed the fall of the Goddard plane in that vicious battle have passed away, meaning that the story of that winter's midday has come to be second- and even third-hand, losing some of its vividness and emotional intensity. Still, after twenty-three years, Jiri recalled his youthful excavation and the satisfaction he felt in knowing some positive steps were actually taken.

One of those positive steps was to write a self-published book in Czech with another local history researcher, Karel Foud, called *Operace Argument*. This book explores all three bomber crashes that occurred in the Plzen region during Big Week. The book's title is the Czech translation of "Operation Argument," which was the code name for the series of bombing missions in February 1944 that eventually became known as Big Week. Jiri Kolouch's findings have helped inspire and inform every ceremony, every monument and every museum about the crash ever since. He is happy that ten families back in the United States know more now than before about "what happened to their boys," providing more closure than they'd had for years. Jiri's excavation uncovered the dog tags of Wayne Nelson, whose loss left the "hole in our family" that led John Torrison to the hole on Dubec Hill. And Ray Noury, the airman hanging from that parachute Jiri's grandmother and others spotted, could make two pilgrimages to the place his buddies had died. These trips, said Jiri, were equal parts sorrow and joy, visits he and the rest of the villagers will include in their narration about what happened on Dubec Hill on February 22, 1944.

There is one final, profound satisfaction to all the villagers' decades of faithful remembering. "My six-year-old son is very interested in this event," Jiri said. The next generation will remember.

Jiri's observations prompted me to consider the reasons for calling Ray, for asking questions, for finding out what happened to Miss Fortune's crew. I knew my own initial motivation well enough, my search for a better understanding of a guarded man—and, possibly, a measure of atonement for the distance I did not try harder to bridge before my father died. But what explained the actions of people like Jiri Kolouch and John Torrison, who toiled to uncover information about people they never met?

I put the question to John. He responded: "I've never sat down and asked, 'What am I looking for?'" He continued, "You just go with the story, see where it goes. I'm not really trying to find an answer to a specific question." Later, he offered a quote about the power of remembering from Tim O'Brien's book, *The Things They Carried,* an account of an infantry company in Vietnam. "And sometimes remembering will lead to a story, which makes it forever. That's what stories are for. Stories are for joining the past to the future." Perhaps John, Jiri and Jiri's grandmother reached the same conclusion as O'Brien's book: "Stories are for eternity, when memory is erased, when there is nothing to remember except the story."

What began for me as a personal inquiry into family history took on greater urgency as I continued to learn more, and as I started to grasp just how committed the people of Nepomuk and surrounding villages were to remembering the story of Miss Fortune. There was much more to know beyond the highs and lows of one father-son relationship.

GEORGE TORRISON, RAY NOURY, AND JOHN TORRISON
AT COMMEMORATION IN NEPOMUK IN 2004.

CHAPTER NINE

COMMEMORATIONS

2004

By the summer and fall of 2003, plans started to come together for Ray to pay his first visit to Nepomuk and Pradlo since falling out of the sky six decades earlier. He had been in contact with Jiri Kolouch about his efforts to excavate the Dubec Hill site and organize the items he found into some kind of museum exhibit. In addition, John and George Torrison had been in contact with Jiri about the exhibit and with Ray about the feelings such efforts brought up for him. A trip to the place might lead to many things, all the men decided—some form of what had come to be known as closure, along with a chance for Ray to express his feelings about the crew and the people of the villages before the opportunity passed.

"The whole story had changed," John recalled, "from George and I just wanting to meet a man who had flown with Wayne and learn about their last mission into finding out that memorials were dedicated to the crew by Czech villagers, who had remembered their liberators. It was unbelievable and something I wanted to understand and experience." On top of all that, John had come to trust

RAY NOURY RECEIVES BOUTONNIERE FROM CZECH GIRL DURING
COMMEMORATION CEREMONIES IN NEPOMUK IN 2009.

Jiri, placing his faith in what the young man was devoting so much of his time and energy to doing. Jiri had, after all, returned one of Wayne's dog tags to John at his own expense after uncovering them at the crash site. These John presented to George on his brother's 70th birthday. Jiri had also sent John photos of visits to the exhibit paid by the American ambassador and the Czech president.

Nothing was certain about the trip, however, even what Ray's reaction to the visit would be. He was an older man by this point, and his health had been anything but good. In addition to his tiny stature, he had come to seem frail. Sitting or standing often required assistance. His speech tended to come in sporadic little bursts, separated by breathing and the struggle to remember. The journey would be long, starting with the transatlantic flight to Prague.

By December 2003, Ray was working out the trip's details. As the sixtieth anniversary of the crash neared, John drove to Rhode Island to pick up Ray then on to JFK Airport in New York to rendezvous with George, who flew in from Denver. They took a direct flight on Czech Airlines to Prague. Ray was happy but visibly nervous. He later gave voice to his uncertainty, asking John, "Who am

I, after sixty years, to go back when most of the people there are all gone."

As is clear to anyone watching videos of the 2004 visit and then of his return in 2009, Ray grew into the role. To this day, the number of people around Nepomuk and Pradlo who insist Ray was a "rock star" is impressive. Yet if that slightly inappropriate term is meant to imply a vision of self-satisfied celebrity, nothing could be further from the truth. Even after Ray received a key to the city and was named as an honorary citizen, he brought a touching humility to his place in the saga of Miss Fortune. He never failed to mention that surviving when all others perished gave him the sacred responsibility to speak not only for himself but for them.

Viewed today, the two-plus hours of edited video present a kaleidoscope of small-town pomp and circumstance, a visit staged to include many speeches and presentations in Czech and English. Thanks to the presence of the Czech military, there is a decided martial air to the proceedings, not to mention the dual flags flown from virtually every public and private building and the dual national anthems performed by a military band. As would become more prevalent in the years that followed, there also was a vintage U.S. Army presence, in 2004 little more than an American Jeep parked near the ceremonies. By the time I visited Nepomuk for the seventieth anniversary of Miss Fortune's last mission in February 2014, the vintage presence had grown to include a full scale army of "reenactors" in period uniforms with period transports, tanks and artillery.

Highlights of Ray's and the Torrison brothers' first visit took place in three quite distinct locations: the square in front of the Mestsky Urad (Town Hall) in the center of Nepomuk; the much smaller village of Pradlo, including the cemetery where the remains of the crew were first buried by villagers; and the hillside crash site itself.

The crash site's appearance has changed somewhat over the years. An initial memorial stone bearing the crew's names was erected in 1997. A new memorial featuring ten granite stones, an obelisk and a new cross was erected in 2009. One thing that has not changed is the presence of a large depression in the soil of Dubec Hill marking the point of impact. Throughout the years, no matter what the status of crew memorials, that depression would remain the starkest monument of them all.

The most public of the ceremonies took place outside the Town Hall, where Ray was made an honorary citizen of Nepomuk. "I receive this," he told Mayor Pavel Jiran, "in honor of all my comrades who died on this mission trying to help people in need." It was a theme he'd return to again and again during the visit. Apparently he had, in his heart, answered the searing question from the flight: Who am I? He was a man allowed by "the good Lord" to speak on behalf of those who were silenced. "I came here," Ray said in a separate speech, "to pay respect to my comrades who fell here in your territory, in the Czech Republic. I'm not a politician, so perhaps I can't find the extra words that most of them use. But I'm sure that the good Lord up above will look upon you and give you the love that everyone needs." Ray went on to express the unity and close-knit sense of family he saw gathered around him. "I would be happy to live here among you," Ray said.

Other key players entered the story at this juncture; they included Pavel Jiran, who was Nepomuk's mayor at the time; Jim Frank from Portland, Oregon, who returned to his native village after escaping from the communists in 1950; and local distiller Petr Jencik, who is seen helping Ray turn to greet someone, sit or rise, or simply get where he needs to get. In scene after scene, Jencik's hulking and bearded presence, complete with necktie within a black leather jacket, is, along with the Torrisons, Ray's entourage.

A large portion of the Nepomuk ceremony consisted of military officers and elected officials laying flowers, from small bouquets to large wreaths, against the outer wall of the municipal building, only feet beneath the plaque commemorating the arrival of George Patton's armies here in May 1945 and the competing arrival of the Soviets. Neither for the first nor last time during the visit did Ray express the wish that Patton had been allowed to take and "keep" Czechoslovakia, as that would have spared the Czech people four decades of communist oppression. And virtually every time Ray spoke, every time he received a compliment, a proclamation or a gift, he touched his shaky fingers to the side of his head in military salute.

During Ray's remarks in Nepomuk—from the major event in the square to a series of small receptions—another theme emerged: his belief that his own countrymen back home should remember and honor World War II veterans (and, by association, all who have served in wartime) the way the people of these villages were doing. There seems to be a confusion and near-exasperation in his verbalized feelings, as though he's amazed by the situation. Addressing his new Czech friends amid the trappings of their still-new freedom, Ray said, "I wish the world would feel the same way as I do, to find that these people who've suffered such hardships never forgot us. I wish Americans would have the same heartfelt devotion to their military."

The ceremonies in Pradlo and on Dubec Hill were much smaller in scale and attendance but their intimacy made them even more affecting. Villagers lined the single road into and out of Pradlo, each bundled against a cold that was biting despite the bright sunshine, waiting for the vintage Jeep that started the procession. Accompanied by the Torrisons and Jencik the distiller, Ray was welcomed to the town by Pradlo Mayor Vaclav Rojik. Rojik drew a respectful laugh from spectators when he told Ray, "We hope the conditions here will be much different for you than they were sixty years ago." Ray's response was simple and direct: "My heart is full of joy." Two young women in traditional village dress performed the traditional Czech "bread and salt" ceremony, a sign of welcome and lasting friendship.

When Ray visited the crash site for the first time since he had landed in a snowdrift a mile or more away, he saw the earth dip into a crater of mud and dead leaves. He saw the stone cross and the square stone plaque listing his name with those of the men who died.

"Unfortunately," Jencik says, referring to the communists' obliteration of the past, "this should have been here in 1946."

"I wish it had been," Ray responded.

"People remembered it," came Jencik's reply, "at least in their hearts."

One of the most spirited exchanges occurred when a man older than most of those present except Ray walked up and started talking about efforts at commemoration going back to 1960. Identifying himself as a former mayor of Pradlo, he insisted there were small, almost underground celebrations going back at least that far, which at least explains why the eventual excavations would be carried out by teenagers who'd heard intriguing stories from their elders. The man talked rapidly, despite the efforts of a translator to stop him and give Ray the English version. At one point, Ray himself picked out the name "Patton," which clearly continued to reverberate through the Czech understanding of their country's ordeal.

"We would have done you more justice much earlier," Ray told the man. "He didn't care for the Russians to take over anything."

There were many more noteworthy encounters during Ray's visit, including a switch on Ray's part to speaking French. He'd, of course, grown up fluent in the language and was happy to discover Petr Jencik was too. Still, that didn't mean English speakers weren't entirely left in the dark when Ray offered his comments in French to Jencik, who then dutifully translated them into Czech. They were probably the only two people in the room who spoke French to any significant degree.

There was a quiet visit to the battered pieces of Miss Fortune, excavated and organized by Jiri Kolouch. There were several receptions, one that featured Ray dancing stiffly as the crowd sang along in Czech and English to an accordion version of the Beer Barrel Polka. There were copious amounts of draft beer consumed, and there was a presentation, by the Kolouchs, of a collection of polished .50-caliber bullets recovered from the crash site. The color was shiny and new. The shapes were beaten, broken and crushed. Clearly, the presenters saw this as a special gift for a special man.

Many in attendance that day would remember above all a brief prayer said at the crash site, the kind of prayer that had been forbidden in this fervently religious land for so long. Ray held his hand over his heart as the words were spoken in Czech, then made the sign of the cross when they ended. He was standing alongside the weathered stone cross, the dark hole in the earth visible beyond his stooped left shoulder. In this moment, Ray confronted the full weight of having survived—of being the only survivor from that day. One came home. Ten did not. And then, six decades later, the one came to the exact spot where Miss Fortune's luck ran out and the double meaning of their plane's chosen nickname became fully apparent. It would not be Ray's last visit to the place where life, death, past and present intersected for Miss Fortune's crew.

2009

Ray was able to pay a second and final visit to those he invariably called "you wonderful people"—the people whose ancestors, as Ray came to see things, had risked everything to save his life. The two visits could not have been more different, even beyond the failing health that forced Ray to move from one ceremony to another with the help of a thick bentwood cane. For one thing, the civilian clothing he wore in 2004 had been replaced by his World War II uniform, with two rows of colorful medals across his chest. For another thing the season was different, early May instead of late February, as the villages commemorated not the downing of an Allied plane but their liberation from the Nazis in May 1945. And finally, Ray on this occasion was the guest of honor at the dedication of a fully realized memorial at the crash site honoring his ten buddies who died there.

CZECHS GATHER AT THE DUBEC HILL CRASH SITE MEMORIAL IN 2009.

The memorial had been in the planning stages for quite some time. It was unclear then, and remains unclear now, exactly who Nepomuk expected to come visit the memorial on any regular basis, since the area's auto travelers clearly prefer the Church of St. John in town and a series of castles atop the hills. The crash site does turn up on a handful on itineraries for bicycle touring, yet there is no apparently financial gain in having such travelers make a quick tour to gaze at a hole in the ground. No, it was simply a growing belief, first among the leadership of Pradlo and then of their counterparts in Nepomuk, that some more organized and impressive recognition was required.

As with any such project, once a commitment exists, there are two main tasks: designing a memorial and raising the money required to build it. For the first, the leadership sought out Czech sculptor Vaclav Fiala, who showed a deep interest in taking on the work. Fiala visited the site, observed the crater and the stone monuments around it—which would remain. In retrospect, he seems to have fixated on the ground, that hard frozen ground that on a long-ago February afternoon provided such a cruel embrace to Miss Fortune and its crew. Then there was the sky, slate gray on that winter's day, and the trees that grew toward the sky, connecting the two elemental forces that, on that day, ushered the men into another realm. In sketches and descriptions, a concept began to emerge.

Fiala understood that the men's remains had been buried together at the first and would be remain so forever. Something individual would be important, he felt, slowly envisioning ten square granite blocks in a straight row across the ground. And just as the trees connected earth and sky, Fiala settled on a leaning obelisk rising only a few feet behind the crater dug by the plane. In perhaps the memorial's most unexpected and striking touch, he made the obelisk reflective on all four sides. Thus, in the dead of winter, the upright slash disappears among bare trees, muddy black ground and leaden skies. In spring, it disappears among bright green leaves and patches of blue sky. What the monument does best, to this day, is disappear. It becomes a reflection of whatever the earth and air and water create around it—like history, like memory. The memorial on Dubec Hill is not about catching or impressing the eye with design prowess; it is about the reality of remembrance.

Ray was excited on several levels to take part in the dedication. The May event took the form of a Liberation Festival, and could be counted on to attract many U.S. veterans, especially Army vets who moved into the region behind Patton in the waning days of the war. As much as he missed his buddies, Ray had come to understand, or at least yearn for, the consolation offered by men who had lived as long as he had and who had, many as mere teenagers, passed through this fiery crucible together. His encounters with aging GIs during the festival were all first-time meetings, but the men acted as though they'd known each other forever.

Many aspects of his first trip were revisited and replayed during his second, often with official speeches that were almost verbatim. What was different was Ray himself. Gone was the uncertainty of that first transatlantic flight, that sense of unworthiness for the task ahead, not to mention the understandable fear of not knowing how well he could handle all the meeting, greeting and speaking. He had done it in 2004, and he could simply do it again, seeing old friends and making new ones. The festival, especially the well-attended festivities in Nepomuk, would help him make many of these new friends.

Although still and video cameras were nothing new to Ray by this point, he and John Torrison also traveled to the Czech Republic with Paul Comire, a man who had visited with Ray at home in Rhode Island, and Friar Didicus of the Franciscan religious order who was interested in interviewing Ray during his return to Nepomuk for the a video series called "Air Maria." Being religious media, these videos focused on Ray's faith and his sense of God's deliverance when his ten friends all died.

Ray and Paul stayed awake all through the night talking, as the first plane made its way from Newark to London and then another from London to Prague. In Prague, the pilot learned of Ray's story and invited him to enter the cockpit and sit to gain a feeling for how far aviation had advanced in more than six decades.

The return visit also included a ceremonial element from Rhode Island. The governor sent proclamations thanking all involved for building Vaclav Fiala's memorial. The local mayors reciprocated. "You are a member of Pradlo forever," Mayor Rojik told Ray, "just as though you were born here. You will always be part of the people."

Another highlight was the visit at the home of Jiri Kolouch Sr., the father of crash-site excavator and amateur historian Jiri Jr. Because he spoke far better English than his father, Jiri Jr. played host to the party. Still, father and son collaborated as best they could, showing Ray the twisted and burned items they'd collected during their excavation of the crash site. They pointed out all or part of three engines, pieces of propeller, pieces of landing gear, an oxygen bottle, several dog tags bearing the fliers' names, a medal showing the Blessed Virgin Mary, even a bent machine gun that rested atop an armoire like the world's grimmest work of decorative art. Within a few years, all these items and more would find their way from Jiri Sr.'s home into the museum on the square in Nepomuk.

Two separate ceremonies honored Ray in 2009—one small and one large. The larger took place in Nepomuk's town square, surrounded by American veterans and re-enactors in period uniforms, the two Jeeps of the ceremony five years earlier now accompanied by transports and MP motorcycles, as vintage U.S. fighters roared by overhead. From a chair positioned in front of a bandstand, Ray spoke from his heart. "I never thought that I could make it after five years to be welcomed here. My heart is full of joy. And you wonderful people welcomed me with open arms. What else could I say but thank you?"

The smaller ceremony took place in the village of Pradlo, led by Mayor Vaclav Rojik. Ray and Rojik made their way around the village with Jim Frank, the Czech expatriate in Oregon, handling translations from Czech into English, or in some cases vice versa. Having learned in 2004 how difficult and awkward the process could be, this time there were prepared remarks, one copy for Ray and one copy for Jim. Traveling from spot to spot by horse drawn carriage—through streets lined by happy celebrants, some in traditional dress—the party laid wreaths at the village cemetery and then at a simple memorial listing the names of the crew nearby. At many stops along the way to the Dubec Hill crash site, remembering his buddies—but also, apparently, aware this might be his last visit—Ray seemed on the verge of tears.

"Whether I come back or not, only God knows," Ray told the gathered crowd at one point. "It's up to Him. And I hope I am able to." Elsewhere, Ray said, "You wonderful people of Czechoslovakia (old names die hard), I want to thank you for honoring me and my former crewmen who paid the highest sacrifice."

VILLAGERS EXAMINE MISS FORTUNE'S WRECKAGE ON DUBEC HILL ON FEBRUARY 22, 1944.

CHAPTER TEN

ECHOES FROM
A HILLSIDE

N epomuk was the kind of market town that grew up across Europe during the Middle Ages, often as much by accident as planning. Wars were fought, kings were unseated, borders were redrawn—but what really kept people alive was farming. And people needed a place they could reach to trade what they could grow or make with whatever they couldn't. Paths through valleys, forests and fields developed simply from people walking along them, and eventually towns developed where they walked. The paths became wider dirt roads, and before long there were carriages making the trip. It was not a leisurely life in or around Nepomuk, ever. To this day, the church bells start ringing every quarter-hour at 5 a.m., as if to remind all that God's up and working and they should be too.

Since the Iron Curtain fell, a portion of the work conducted in Nepomuk has focused on creating sites recognizing Miss Fortune's crew. Like the monument on Dubec Hill itself, these commemoration sites in Nepomuk and other villages near the hill have evolved over time. A cross appeared during the winter of 1989-1990 at the crew's crash site on Dubec Hill, followed by a memorial stone in 1997. A wooden plaque was mounted near the village of Blovice in 1991; it bore an inscription stating, "They Braved the Storm, We Might Have the Sun." Small exhibitions of artifacts from the crash site were held in 2000 and from 2003-2005; these were followed by the creation of a permanent, room-sized museum exhibit in a building near Nepomuk's town square, which opened in 2014.

Before the town honored the crew of Miss Fortune in a permanent way in 2014, there was another reason a modern traveler might make his way to Nepomuk—whether by car or catching the regional Ceske Drahy train from Prague's main station to Plzen and then, since the track was usually being worked on, a bus from there to the station in Nepomuk. The main hotel in Nepomuk is called U Zeleneho stromu, or simply "Hotel Nepomuk," and is located on the town's main square. It houses an outlet of the Svejk restaurant chain that crops up here and there around the Czech Republic. The chain's logo, borrowed from the satirical World War I antiwar novel *The Good Soldier Svejk,* is omnipresent.

A map atop the front desk provides an icy geography lesson, especially for those with any sense of 20th century history. There is today's Czech Republic—the land of the Prague Spring of 1968, resisting then falling victim to the Soviet Army, the land of the Velvet Revolution in 1989 that chose poet-playwright Vaclav Havel as the new country's first president—still hemmed in by Germany to the west and Austria to the south. In 1938, much of this border country was called (by Germans, never by Czechs) Sudetenland, and after absorption of his native Austria, Hitler turned his hungry gaze here and launched what is now known as World War II. On this hotel map, one highway heading west from the Czech Republic via Plzen is marked by its nearest major destination: Regensburg.

While it may require a car, a bike or a strong pair of legs to reach Miss Fortune's crash site from the Nepomuk town square, it's only the briefest of strolls to the town's other landmark—the Church of St. John of Nepomuk. St. John was born about 1340 in Pomuk (and Nepomuk means "Not Pomuk"), but Pomuk doesn't exist anymore. John was known as a holy man in his day, coming from a family of education and eventually rising into the Catholic Church's hierarchy in Prague. This, ultimately, led to his being tortured and killed.

John backed the archbishop in a power struggle with King Wenceslaus IV (not the first "Good King Wenceslaus" of Christmas carol fame) and refused to tell the king what the queen had shared during her confessions. According to one Nepomuk brochure in English, "Just keeping secret of the confession resulted in the king's raving hate. This shows above all the king's unprecedented activity in the torture chamber. He himself burnt John's side with a torch in order to find out all necessary facts." John died from this torture, his body tossed into the Vltava River from a spot on Prague's famed Charles Bridge that's now marked by his statue. The saint is sometimes depicted with a finger in front of his mouth and a crown of five stars, one for each of the wounds suffered by Jesus, for each of the fishermen who found John's body in the Vltava, and for each of the letters in the Latin word *tacui* (meaning "I kept silent.")

Today's Church of St. John of Nepomuk is the best part of any view from the square or the Hotel Nepomuk. It was built after the saint's death on the site reputed to be his parents' home. The land had held a church for centuries (dedicated to a different John, the wild-eyed Baptizer of the River Jordan), starting out Romanesque and then going Gothic when that became the trend. A fire destroyed those early edifices and today's colorful (shades of yellow, peach and terra cotta), twin-spired Baroque wonder took their place.

The town of Nepomuk traditionally welcomed visitors at least twice a year, when large numbers of pilgrims, including church dignitaries and notables, made their way here for feasts associated with the birth and death of both St. Johns. Such travelers could be expected to visit the town's other religious sites as well, from the Church of St. Jacob/James to its nearby Archdeanery to the Column of St. Adalbert. With the establishment of a permanent museum exhibit devoted to Miss Fortune's crew in 2014, visitors on these and any other days might be interested in adding a more recent commemoration to their Nepomuk itinerary.

I visited the Nepomuk museum exhibit during its grand opening in February 2014, which was timed to coincide with the seventieth anniversary of Miss Fortune's last mission. As I examined the display cases, photographs and large pieces of Miss Fortune's engines, I wondered why so much effort had gone into creating this museum in a rural corner of the Czech Republic. The crash of one B-24 Liberator during World War II—indeed, World War II itself—is ancient history to many Americans, who feel no more personal connection to the events of 1944 than they do to the events of 1864 or 1764. And yet, the explosion that marked the death of ten U.S. airmen on Dubec Hill continues to echo through the streets of Nepomuk and surrounding villages seven decades later.

MEMORIAL IN PRADLO, WHERE THE CREW'S REMAINS WERE FIRST BURIED IMMEDIATELY AFTER THE CRASH.

A partial answer to my question emerged in the form of two men who became driving forces behind efforts to commemorate Miss Fortune's crew: Jim Frank and Pavel Jiran.

Jim Frank entered John Torrison's field of vision when Jim served as Ray Noury's translator during Ray's 2004 trip to Nepomuk. Jim was visiting his sister in a nearby village at the time, heard about Ray's upcoming visit, and decided to stay longer to meet him. In truth, however, Jim's connection to the crew goes back much farther.

Although Jim has lived in Portland, Oregon since 1950, he retains the slight rumble of a Czech accent. His roots lie in the tiny village of Kahradka not far from Dubec Hill. He was a significant force in memorializing the crew and the crash site with the 2004 ceremony and the physical memorial five years later. Born in 1930, Jim was fourteen when Miss Fortune crashed.

"We never saw or heard anything in our village," Jim remembered at age eighty-four. "But we heard about it immediately. The thing is, at first we were told the plane was British. Eventually we understood it was American. We were told it was forbidden to come to the crash site, that the German army was already there."

Jim didn't actually visit the crash site until 1970. He had escaped from behind the Iron Curtain and spent two and a half years in a refugee camp in Italy. There, he met and married his Prague-born wife and the first of their five children was born. The family made its way to America with nothing. By 1970, he was established in his new country with a successful construction company in Portland. It was his first visit back to what was still called Czechoslovakia and still run according to the whims of Moscow. The visit came only two years after the Prague Spring and the horrors that had followed. Visiting the crash site, Jim was moved, both as a Czech and as an American. He was assured by his relatives there was nothing to be done, that the Russians wouldn't allow any memorial and indeed prohibited any mention of America's role in the defeat of Nazi Germany. To the Russians, it was the Great War. Their Great War.

As long as the communists were in charge in Prague, Jim knew there would be no Dubec Hill memorial to the sacrifices made by young men from his adopted homeland. Yet from hardships he'd experienced in his life, he also knew he couldn't forget what had happened.

"I dearly wanted to expose the total impact that this had on those families, on the mothers when they lost their sons," said Jim. "People should know the human side of the story. When I first came to Portland in 1950, I met two Czech families. One of their sons had died in the war in Europe, the other in the Pacific. I met the mothers. The impact of their loss on me was beyond words."

The conviction that something needed to done on Dubec Hill was never far from Jim's mind, even as he concentrated on his family and his career in America. Jim was always good with his hands. He had worked making furniture in Plzen before the 1948 communist takeover. When the sponsors who initially brought the family to Portland went bankrupt, the Franks were taken into the care of a local Catholic priest, and from there Jim found a job in a cabinet shop. Jim might have remained there forever had it not been for the union. Jim had a major problem with that element of American life. He quit the cabinet shop and launched a business of his own, moving in time from building cabinets to handling small home remodeling to eventually building complete houses. "Virtually all the architects in Portland came to us with work," Jim recalled. "They really passed our name around."

With his sister still living in Nepomuk, and his niece eventually married to town Mayor Pavel Jiran, Jim kept up with progress after the fall of communism. Almost as soon as the staunchly anti-religious Soviets left the country, people of the surrounding villages erected a simple stone memorial with a crucifix at the crash site. Shortly after the start of the new millennium, talk got serious—somebody should raise money to design and build a real memorial. Jim agreed to help.

He raised funds for the project, calling mostly on Czech-American families he knew in Portland. He participated in the design with artist Vaclav Fiala, though, to his disappointment, the five-pointed Air Corps star from the original proposal he advocated did not make it atop the leaning obelisk. And he was there on the hill for both dedications in 2004 and 2009. At both of these ceremonies, Jim's two lives and two languages came together as he served as translator for Ray Noury. Having spoken mostly English for so many decades, he admittted the task in Czech had not been an easy one.

"It was so moving to be here for that," Jim said. "Both times Ray came to the site, he went right to the stone with the crucifix on it and knelt down and prayed. Then he started speaking, and that was when my trouble started. I just couldn't think of all the words in Czech, though people all applauded at the end and I guess it was fine. But Ray said so much from his heart, and he kept talking. He just couldn't help himself. He kept saying how much he loved everybody."

Not long before Ray's death, Jim visited him in Rhode Island. Like John Torrison and I experienced, Jim found Ray to be quick in terms of thinking and speaking, despite the health issues that come with advancing years. As far as Jim was concerned, Ray still had a "brilliant mind" and a "vivid memory" of all the things that had befallen him. Ray especially remembered the kindness he had been shown by strangers risking Nazi retaliation by doing anything to help a freshly downed U.S. airman who, earlier that morning, had been busy bombing Germany.

"I wanted," said Jim, "to be part of thanking America for the liberation and to be part of the memory of these people that gave their lives. In 2004, one comment I heard really sticks in my mind. The villagers said these young boys came so far to bring us freedom."

A similar sentiment runs through the comments of Pavel Jiran, who served as my host when I visited the museum and crash site in 2014. Pavel was the mayor of Nepomuk when the first plans were made to create a permanent memorial in 2004; the vice mayor when the finished memorial was dedicated in 2009; and a member of the Town Council when the permanent museum was opened in 2014. But Pavel knew nothing about the crash on Dubec Hill until he moved here with his wife in 1992. His father-in-law had recently passed away, and the couple relocated from Prague to be closer to the widow. It was a relocation that changed everything.

As is typical of a leader in a small town, the man isn't a politician for a living. Born in Prague but then taken to live here and there throughout childhood by a father in the Czech military—an "Army brat," in American parlance—Pavel grew up wanting to be an engineer. He had a strong interest in the electrical side of that profession but ended up studying mining, the main industry in several parts of then-Czechoslovakia where he had lived. To this day, he works full time as a mining engineer, handling Nepomuk business on the side between trips to the office in Plzen or virtually anywhere in the country his skills are needed.

Pavel, who is Jim Frank's nephew by marriage, never was fascinated by World War II. After his stint as mayor of Nepomuk, however, Pavel has accumulated an over-filled five-inch-thick binder of photos, drawings, historical documents, news clippings and mementos relating to Miss Fortune's final landing. Having served as the "face of Nepomuk" for several key ceremonies, he treasures many photos of himself with Ray Noury in the villages—and even a few with General George S. Patton's grandson.

"I knew that every year on February 22, there were commemorations with veterans," Pavel says of the situation when he arrived in Nepomuk. "It was the first time I'd known anything about the Liberator or what happened here. It was very interesting to me. I knew about the parts of the plane being kept at Jiri Kolouch's house, and I went there to look at these parts."

As the story goes, Pavel didn't speak a lot of English when the town began uncovering Miss Fortune's story. But as American veterans and modern-day American military members have come to pay tribute at the site on Dubec Hill, he's been using the language more and more. Now he functions quite well in English—giving speeches, attending receptions, serving as an important link between the Americans who've come to feel so much for the site and the locals who've held such feeling for it since 1944.

Pavel worked with Jiri Kolouch on trying to track down the crew's sole survivor, finally zeroing in on Ray's residence in Rhode Island. And Pavel took part in the first phone call, explaining to Ray who his callers were, where they were and why they were calling. As Pavel remembers it, the call did not go well. Ray explained that his health was bad and that all these things they were talking about had happened a long, long time ago. The parties agreed to speak again, and they did. Ray's health had improved and the Nepomuk group asked him to come to Nepomuk for the crash's sixtieth anniversary. Pavel was waiting at Prague Airport when Ray came off the plane, accompanied by John and George Torrison.

"I organized all things around the memory," said Pavel. "As we got more information about the crew, its eleven people—one alive, ten dead—I kept asking for new information. I think it's very necessary for people of this town. It was hard but it was very good work for me. The contact with Ray and the Torrisons touched my heart. It was friendship from the first, forever."

This friendship deepened long-distance between Ray's first visit and his second. And it continued when Pavel helped Nepomuk decide to move the plane's mangled parts from Jiri Kolouch's home to a small, temporary space in the town museum. As the collection grew, having at last found a resting place, the idea of a larger exhibition upstairs took root. Pieces were curated, facts were checked and rechecked, organization of information was discussed, all leading to the opening of a permanent display for the seventieth anniversary in 2014. Driven mostly by his affection for Ray Noury and Ray's obvious warm feelings for the town that had saved his life, Pavel participated in each milestone.

Paging through his bulging binder, Pavel stopped and smiled, or shared a story, when he encountered a picture of Ray in Nepomuk—Ray signing autographs, Ray shaking hands with someone from the village, Ray giving a speech in the square, Ray holding his hand over his heart for the national anthem. Pavel's elderly American friend had traveled a long road to experience these remembrances, and he'd traveled it with the Torrisons at his side, along with all the people of Nepomuk in spirit. Most of all, Ray had traveled it with a town mayor who came to believe that what happened on that hillside in 1944 should never be forgotten. "It changed my life," Pavel said.

In a sense, I suppose, Miss Fortune's last mission became Pavel's mission—and, by extension, the town's mission. Pavel honored the sacrifice; got to know Ray as the embodiment of the crew's courage; and worked hard to make sure their story would be told. After I met Pavel in Nepomuk and participated in the 2014 commemoration, I realized that I had packed more than I needed for the day's activities. I received a list of events with several entries including morning Mass; speeches in the town center; a wreath-laying ceremony at the crash site; and a ribbon-cutting ceremony at the museum exhibit. The list did not include making amends or unlocking secrets. In fact, although the events on my list were worded in various ways, they all identified the same basic activity: showing gratitude.

CRASH WITNESSES PANI KROUPOVA AND VACLAV BANACEK.

CHAPTER ELEVEN

VILLAGE VOICES

My mother always maintained that being transferred to United's Denver hub in 1951 was good medicine for my father. While the move did not tame his temper or heal his ulcers, it did allow him some distance from an array of bad memories that had accumulated in Washington D.C. Like many others in post-war America, my parents left their home towns, moved west and launched busy new lives that no doubt differed from what they had envisioned for themselves on December 6, 1941.

I thought about the frenzied pace of change in post-war America as I considered another task to accomplish in Nepomuk—locating eyewitnesses to Miss Fortune's crash on Dubec Hill. If Denver embodies change, then Nepomuk embodies the opposite quality. The "new" church in town is hundreds of years old. People stay put. And when a town's history is measured in centuries, exploring events that occurred seventy years ago does not seem like such a long trek into the past after all.

I stayed in the hotel called U Zeleneho Stromu on the square in Nepomuk. Jim Frank and Pavel Jiran used it as the location for setting up interviews with eyewitnesses Pani Kroupova, who searched for bodies in Miss Fortune's wreckage, and Vaclav Banacek, who watched as the mortally wounded B-24 lost altitude over Pradlo just before it crashed. Although they were not eyewitnesses themselves, Karel Foud, Milan Demela and Jaromir Ruzicka also provided additional details about Miss Fortune's last moments and the aftermath.

The hotel is a perfect place to contemplate the past, not least because it has developed its own rich history since its construction in 1909. Jim Frank remembered stopping there for a beer with his father seven decades ago when they came in from their village to sell a cow. He still remembered the painting on the wall in the restaurant. In its sunny breakfast room, photos of somber-looking men bottling beer in the building on August 24, 1944 were taken just seven months after Miss Fortune fell out of the sky to crash on Dubec Hill.

It was a long war, longer in Czechoslovakia than anywhere else in Europe, and though the Allies had landed in Normandy two months earlier, the final outcome was anything but certain. There were Nazis around every corner in Nepomuk and a thousand other towns just like it, Wehrmacht soldiers in uniform or Gestapo men in trench coats and their numberless spies, always ready to torture for information or blind retribution. Determined to obliterate any sense of Czech nationality, the Nazis had been brutal to the citizenry. These men making beer and filling bottles in the photo had every reason to be somber.

The crash of an American bomber was more than a startling and disturbing event for the people who lived near Nepomuk. The presence of a downed airman introduced elements of risk and choice that the villagers understood only too well in light of their knowledge of the fate that befell a place called Lidice.

Like Nepomuk, Lidice had been a typical Czech village of men, women and children; homes and businesses; and a church from the 14th century. On June 10, 1942, Hitler ordered his Gestapo to destroy Lidice in unimaginably brutal ways because of the mistaken belief that men from the town had been involved in the assassination of the Protektor, Reinhard Heydrich.

When the Nazis occupied Czechoslovakia in 1939, Hitler imposed a "Protectorate"—one of the earliest examples of Nazi perversion of language. Other than sparing Prague (as even the Russians would do at the end of the Cold War four decades later), very little about Czechoslovakia would be protected in the coming years. The Protektor arrived in 1941 and set the dreadful story motion.

During his time as Reich Protector over the Czech people at the behest of Adolph Hitler, Heydrich earned many gruesome nicknames, including "The Butcher of Prague." Hitler himself called Heydrich "The Man with the Iron Heart." Before his assassination in 1942, Heydrich had risen to the heights of Nazi power by the methods with which he put down dissent and his far-reaching beliefs about racial and national purity. Many consider him to be a primary architect of the Holocaust.

Heydrich died from wounds he received in an attack on the road. The manhunt was nationwide. Information was required, and the Gestapo certainly knew how to get information. Torture was applied to any Czechs who seemed they might possess a puzzle piece, and many were simply executed—as was the threat made public for anyone harboring almost anything about the fugitives. In all, some thirty-six thousand homes were searched by upwards of twenty-one thousand German soldiers. The destruction of Lidice, and shortly thereafter another village called Lezaky, was planned as part of the manhunt—even though no evidence ever linked either village to any aspect of the conspiracy to assassinate Heydrich.

When the Gestapo moved against Lidice on June 10, 1942, all 173 men over the age of fifteen were gathered and gunned down. Another eleven men missing that day were killed later. In all, 184 women and eighty-eight children were deported to concentration camps, with a few children later deemed Aryan enough in appearance handed over to SS families. In one of the short films shown in the Lidice museum, elderly versions of these children share the experience of growing up as Germans and only later learning the truth. The women were sent to Ravensbruck; eighty-two of the children were sent to the Chelmno extermination camp, never to return. Bodies of villagers who'd already passed away were dug up and mutilated. Even the animals of Lidice, household pets and beasts of burden alike, were slaughtered amidst the frenzy. The Nazis brought in a filmmaker named Franz Treml, a collaborator who had run a Zeiss-Ikon camera shop at the Lucerna Palace in Prague, to record each chilling step of the process and ensure that ensure every single Czech would know what had happened to Lidice.

What the villagers around Dubec Hill must have thought, and the choices they made when they heard the bomber crash and spotted Ray Noury's lone parachute floating down, had everything to do with the fate of Lidice.

PANI KROUPOVA

It is one thing to know or say or write that Miss Fortune crashed into Dubec Hill. It is quite another to learn the details from someone who arrived at the scene while the metal was still hot. That witness is Pani Kroupova, a thin, elderly woman with white hair and a plain dress. I initially thought "Pani" was her first name; I later learned that it is a form of address for an older woman.

Crying twice, Pani Kroupova described her darkest memories of February 22, 1944, when she was an eighth-grader warned to give her country's Nazi occupiers a wide berth. She cried when she recalled her father digging through an American plane's wreckage in search of bodies, and she cried again over a youthful indiscretion. She was only fourteen, and an indiscretion could be forgiven. But she wasn't remembering something she did, really. She was remembering something she saw, and that she continues to see.

Kroupova barely recalled a time before the Nazis came to occupy her village near Pradlo, and the reality of that occupation was omnipresent and cruel. As she ceased to look like a child, her mother issued increasingly stern warnings about not attracting the soldiers' attention. As with many girls coming of age, these warnings preceded any detailed understanding of what her mother was warning against. Kroupova remembers walking home from school with other girls one day when a truck full of soldiers sped up upon them. The vehicle swerved to look like the driver was trying to kill them, and the girls all jumped into a muddy ditch. Her final, lasting memory of the incident was the laughter of the soldiers.

"They thought it was funny," she said.

On February 22, 1944, the teachers led the students down into shelters around lunch time, explaining there were bombers reported in the vicinity, American or British. When they led them out, it was 1:15. Kroupova was sent home to her village, a walk of four kilometers. When she got there, she found her mother crying. Something terrible might have happened, her mother said. The soldiers stationed in the area had come looking for her father. They ordered him to come see something up on Dubec Hill, since he was listed as some sort of health officer. Seeing plumes of smoke rising from the side of Dubec Hill, she decided to follow her father.

Kroupova has never forgotten what she saw: her father, working under the stern eyes of the country's Nazi overlords, lifting pieces of human bodies from pile after pile of mangled metal. She recognized some of the organs from her classes at school, but it still horrified her that her father had to use bits of the plane to help lift body parts large and small from the piles. Kroupova was crying on the hillside by then, and she was crying again seventy years later talking about it.

At one point a soldier walked up to Kroupova's father and pointed to a tree. His father looked and nodded somberly, taking a few moments to tell his daughter that whatever she did, don't go near that tree. In keeping with her age, however, Kroupova did precisely that. She walked to that tree and, pressing its branches from side to side, came face to face with a limb dripping with human intestines. She has always regretted not listening to her father.

"It was a very solemn occasion, even for the German soldiers," said Kroupova, wiping her eyes. "Lots of people cried up on Dubec Hill that afternoon and into the night. It was very sad for most people, especially seeing so many bodies broken up."

She specifically remembers the Nazis leaving the body parts gathered around the plane, and they seemed to have no plan for holding any kind of service or even finding a place to bury them. It was the villagers, she says, who brought together all the human remains and buried them together in the local cemetery. It didn't seem right to do any less, especially since most people around Pradlo held firmly to their Catholic faith. They sneaked back to the crash site after dark and buried the Americans in a single grave in secret. Kroupova doesn't remember the soldiers doing anything to stop them or, later, to punish them.

Beginning almost as soon as communism ended in Czechoslovakia in 1989, Kroupova felt the people of Pradlo unify around the idea of remembering these airmen. There were early ceremonies at the cemetery, even though the bodies had been gone from here a long time. And then there was a stone commemoration plaque at the crash site, listing the names of the ten men who died and the one man who survived.

Kroupova was happy the men were getting the gratitude they deserve, from the people of Pradlo and Nepomuk, and maybe eventually from their own country. She felt the attention and respect for their sacrifice were long overdue. But still, each time there was a ceremony about the events on Dubec Hill, she felt herself dragged back into memories she wishes she could leave behind. She saw it as the price she had to pay for being there on that hill all those years ago, and witnessing all that she witnessed.

"It never left my memories," she observed simply. "It's always alive in my mind, especially at the anniversary." Kroupova looked like she might start crying again, but caught herself and settled down to add, "Very much so."

VACLAV BANACEK

Like Kroupova, Vaclav Banacek also learned important lessons at an early age during World War II.

Even as a fifth grader in a small village outside Pradlo, Vaclav Banacek knew the German SS when he saw it. For one thing, its members wore special insignia, like the SS emblem on their collars that resembled a jagged lightning bolt—lighting was a meaningful description of how the SS operated—or the gruesome laughing skull and crossbones fronting their peaked caps. Young Vaclav also knew the SS because they were the Germans most likely to be pushing Czechs around, threatening them if they didn't do precisely as they were told. Whenever a villager was in trouble, whether arrested or merely questioned and returned, the SS was sure to be involved.

Pradlo, a town only slightly larger but better organized than the surrounding villages, provided young Vaclav with one of his first remembered examples of Nazi terror. It happened at the local distillery.

"The director there was hiding some weapons," the white-haired Vaclav said, sitting beside Kroupova in the bar at the hotel. He started out in a calm voice but became more agitated each time a story touched on Nazi aggression, which was understandable, because each time that aggression came to threaten his own family. "Somebody told on him to the Germans and the soldiers came to the distillery. The man was picked up by the SS and executed. As a result of this, there was a massive search of the entire village, for more hidden weapons of course but also for anything else that was forbidden. Meat was rationed under the Germans. Some of the villagers kept their own pigs in secret, to feed their families. If that meat was found, it was punishable."

As part of this search, an SS officer came to Vaclav's father's butcher shop with a couple of regular soldiers and questioned him at some length. As the old man remembers this moment from his youth, the officer then turned to his mother, said *"Guten tag"* and she answered in German, immediately bringing on the question of whether she was German. No, she answered, she had simply worked in a German hospital and had learned the language. His suspicions apparently satisfied, Vaclav says, the officer gave his family two additional sausages. "Look, you are good people," he said in parting. "The only reason we are doing this is because some-body reported wrongdoing."

Life was austere under Nazi occupation, and terrifying to a degree never experienced there before the war. The villagers never knew what might happen with something they were telling a friend—maybe something casual, even something intended as a joke—and they never knew who might hear something and turn them in to the Nazis. Everyone knew of atrocities. They had heard of Lidice and of a thousand smaller versions that befell a cousin or an uncle.

On February 22, 1944, as Vaclav recalls, he was assigned the afternoon shift at his school in Pradlo. The students were outside right after eating lunch, he says, despite the snowy conditions. It was shortly after 1 p.m. Suddenly they heard something in the sky and looked up to see a large airplane spewing black smoke and perhaps some flames, flying very low and getting lower quickly. The sound was terrible, he says, like roaring, like grinding. And then the plane disappeared behind Dubec Hill. The students all knew it had crashed.

Sent home, Vaclav immediately told his father what he had seen and listened intently to what his father had heard from villagers coming into his butcher shop. Many of them were headed up Dubec Hill to see what they could see. Vaclav's father was heading there too and was willing to take him along.

"There were already German squads around the crash site, but they were not preventing anyone from approaching or even from picking up small items," said Vaclav. "I saw many broken bodies, dismembered bodies. It was a horrible, horrible scene. The plane was still smoking when we got there, with little fires burning all over the ground. The plane was still hot. We could feel the heat on our faces, even on that cold day." Vaclav pondered the memory in silence for a moment, then made a connection across time. "Years later, when I was in high school, I made friends with a boy who had no father. He told me eventually his father at been there, at the crash, and had taken a gold ring from the finger of a dead airman, to keep it away from the Germans. This got to be known, my friend told me, and the Germans took him to a concentration camp. The father was never seen again."

KAREL FOUD

Book author and local historian Karel Foud is an important link for anyone who wants to understand the events that unfolded on Dubec Hill in February 1944.

Throughout the centuries, teenage boys have gotten in trouble with symbols of authority for doing all kinds of things. Few, however, other than Karel Foud of Plzen, have been investigated by the national police for an unhealthy and unpatriotic obsession with the American role in World War II.

Contact with the West was strictly forbidden into the 1980s, with the Czech communist party and its Soviet overlords monitoring any efforts to cut through the Iron Curtain. Young Karel found out anything he could, doggedly pursuing the next piece of information and the one after that. It only pressed him onward to learn that his hometown, Plzen, had been the scene of the last major air attack of the war, an all-out bombing raid on the Skoda armament factory.

"The American bombers became my own personal interest," said Karel, sipping hot tea from a large clear-glass bowl while wearing a GI-green U.S. Army jacket with sleeve insignia proclaiming "92nd Division." When asked if the jacket had special signifigance to his research, he explained "It's just a jacket," with a gentle laugh. "Any interest in the American involvement in these matters was forbidden. I would have been dismissed from college if what I was doing was known. Whatever I did was totally in secret."

Happily for Karel, the departure of the communists after the Velvet Revolution opened the door on two things that he considered essential: the free exchange of World War II information with the U.S. and other governments as well as with veterans themselves, and the liberty to travel to other places that played a big part in the story, such as Germany. Even as Karel finished college and started a career in historic preservation, he got serious about studying the air war in his native Czechoslovakia, including the activities of the Luftwaffe, the RAF from England, and the U.S. Army Air Corps.

Foud wrote his first book, *The Last Mission,* about the Skoda bombing in Plzen. He wrote a later work entitled *500 Hours Toward Victory* about General George S. Patton in the final days of the war. In between these projects, Foud heard about the tragedy on Dubec Hill. He became fascinated with this nearly forgotten event, long suppressed by the communists, and set out to tell the story.

The resulting self-published book, *Operace Argument,* written with Jiri Kolouch of Nepomuk, Vladislav Krayky and Jan Vladar, produced only in Czech and now out-of-print, became for many the bible on Miss Fortune's demise, along with the fate of two other B-24s that crashed in the vicinity on that same day. Finally allowed to move across borders, whether in person or by phone, facsimile, letter or eventually email, Karel was at long last able to learn about the lives and families of the young men who went down with these bombers. In a world where few faced such soul-wrenching choices anymore, and in which good and evil were no longer so clearly demarked, their bravery astounded him.

Maybe he felt he'd lived before in that time, or maybe he merely wished he had. Or maybe Karel was dabbling in another form of historic preservation, that treasures the lives of long-dead human beings the way he treasured buildings, statues and paintings in his day job.

Along the way, between personal visits to legendary American battle sites like the Normandy beaches in France and the Ardennes Forest in Belgium (site of The Battle of the Bulge), Karel made significant discoveries in Germany about the air campaign that was called "Operation Argument." He not only photographed the airfields from which the German pilots launched their fighters, but also found archival paperwork crediting a Liberator destroyed over Czech territory on February 22 to a young pilot named Friedrich Muer. *"Der 6./Z.G. 1 wird der Abschuss eijnes amerikanischen Kampfflugzeuges vom Typ Consilidated 'Liberator' am 22.2.44 12.52..."* says the official German war record. Clearly, this was one of the three B-24s shot down within forty miles of each other. Karel would have tracked down Muer and asked him what he remembered, as he did several other fighter pilots who'd flown for Germany, but Muer had himself been shot down and killed the same day. The pilot's formal yet boyish portrait is included in the book.

"What happened on Dubec Hill might seem small," Karel said, taking the final sip of his tea. "I strived to give each of these airmen a name, to make their names known to the general public, and to make sure their names are never forgotten. These people are not just a number. There's a personal tragedy in every life that's lost."

MILAN DEMELA

During my visit to the 2014 commemoration in Nepomuk, I noticed an ever-present observer who recorded the day's events. If the groundswell of emotion leading to the crew's commemoration had an official photographer, it would be school teacher and amateur photographer Milan Demela. From Ray Noury to Skipper Miller to the visiting grandson of General George S. Patton, Milan, who teaches the Czech language to students at a local trade school, has taken pictures of them all, capturing an important chapter in Nepomuk's history in the process.

In the Miss Fortune exhibit inside the Nepomuk museum, much interest always surrounds the old, scratchy black-and-white photos of people milling around the crash site within days, perhaps within hours of the terrible impact. For all the distortions suffered by the 1944 prints or negatives, there even seems to be smoke rising from the wreckage in some of the shots. Some people gathered are clearly villagers. Others may or may not be in German uniform. Virtually every other photograph in the exhibit, telling the story from 2004 to 2014, is by Demela.

"This was a forgotten matter before Ray's arrival," Milan observed. "I only knew by word-of-mouth that one member of the crew had survived. But we knew nothing about Ray until he arrived."

With thick shocks of silver hair cascading down his forehead and a bushy mustache to match, Milan drank a large cold mug of Pilsener Urquell as he spoke of the forces that took hold of his hobby in the days leading up to Ray's first visit. For all the lack of interest in earlier years—and communist suppression of whatever interest there was—Milan had connections to Dubec Hill that made him a natural for his unexpected vocation.

For one thing, he had heard of the crash while growing up in the nearby village of Mohelnice. His grandfather had been at work that day in Plzen—at the Skoda armament factory, probably constructing wooden models for the foundries to cast metal parts—when word started to spread outward from the hill. As soon as he made it home that evening, Milan's grandfather raced to the site. When he shared this, I wondered if he might be one of those people looking shocked, saddened and confused in one of those old photographs. Milan remembered getting the basic facts of the crash from his grandfather, but he didn't have a way to confirm them until he chatted with Ray Noury in 2004. This the two men did, and Milan was impressed by the accuracy of the conversations he remembered from those first years after his birth in 1958.

Another family connection to Miss Fortune came from Milan's parents, who spoke regularly of American soldiers of the 4th Armored Division who stayed at their house for about a week in the war's final days, as the Red Army closed in from the east. "My parents had such warm memories of those people," Milan says. "Our family still has many mementos of their stay at our house."

Beginning in the months leading up to the sixtieth anniversary of the crash on February 22, 2004, Milan felt his excitement grow. He was already taking still photos of anything or anybody who would let him, and he'd more recently added a video camera to his equipment. After talking over the matter with Pavel Jiran and deciding this event was important for Nepomuk, he decided to chronicle the entire proceedings. When he first met Ray Noury in the middle of a public appearance, he thought the man was a bit overwhelmed.

"He seemed very surprised, almost afraid, not knowing how he would be received. The town all called him the Small Big Man." I mentioned that, in English, the movie title was *Little Big Man,* and Milan laughed and nodded, to say: yes, that's what they called him. "Once Ray knew he was received warmly by the people here, then he really warmed up too." Milan grins from beneath his mustache. "Ray was like a movie star."

As Milan became caught up in the excitement, there was no stopping him. He managed to take both still and video shots of each significant event, sometimes with help from his wife and

SKIPPER GODDARD MILLER AND HER SON, BRAD, LAY A WREATH AT THE MEMORIAL SITE ON DUBEC HILL IN 2005. PAVEL JIRAN LOOKS ON.

daughter. The 2004 hillside ceremony dissolved into the 2009 ceremony with the complete memorial, with Ray as guest of honor for both events along with John Torrison. Milan was especially touched by a visit that was far less public. In 2005, Skipper Miller came to Dubec Hill to see the place her father had lost his life. "It was the most moving experience for her," Milan says, a fact that comes through in his photographs in the exhibition.

By the time Milan found himself shooting the 2009 commemoration and the 2014 museum dedication, an exhibition which features dozens of his photos, Dubec Hill had found a secure place in the hearts and minds of Nepomuk. With Ray Noury having passed away and many other American World War II veterans unlikely to return, these memorials loomed even larger as links to this past. Memories in the villages remained, though fading. And Milan Demela's emotional, colorful photographs strenghthened the trove of memories.

JAROMIR RUZICKA

Although I did not attend the 2004 commemoration with Ray, I heard about one particular moment that featured a cameo by Jaromir Ruzicka.

Born in September 1944, six months after Miss Fortune's crash and nine months before the end of the war, Jaromir Ruzicka insisted he has only one wartime memory—and he admitted he probably got that from his mother. He was in a baby stroller, perhaps on a visit from his village of Srby near Dubec Hill to the big city of Plzen, and he and his mother were hiding beneath a railway bridge near the station as American bombs exploded overhead.

Jaromir stopped short of saying so, but that would place them in Plzen on April 25, 1945, the day the 8th Air Force launched an all-out effort to take out the last major German armament factory: the legendary Skoda works. Jaromir ended up working later beside Jiri Kolouch, the young man who excavated the Miss Fortune crash site, during the communist era. By then, the rebuilt factory was making electric locomotives, spare parts for steam engines and also parts for the same kind of Russian tanks that rolled through the streets of the capital (and onto the world's newscasts) to suppress the freedoms of Prague Spring in 1968.

Thanks to the beloved old woman Jaromir referred to as his "Babichka" (grandmother), he was able to make an even greater contribution to the war effort and its memories around Dubec Hill, six decades after the fact. As the events around Nepomuk attracted attention in late 2003 and early 2004, Jaromir found himself remembering an old story he'd heard when he was about six, and an object attached somehow to that story he'd discovered much more recently. His Babichka, he remembered, had been the very first witness to reach the crash scene, the long, black smoking trench that Miss Fortune had dug into the hillside.

"My grandmother always told me she saw many parts of bodies, some pieces hanging from the trees," Jaromir recounted without emotion. "She told me she went immediately to the place, maybe with another woman, before anyone else from the village or any German soldiers got there. They were just out walking in the woods when the tragedy happened, and they were close. They found a pair of heated gloves at the place, partially burned in the fires that were still burning. And my grandmother took the gloves to her house."

Some years after the war, Jaromir's grandmother moved away from the village and, as he puts it, "nobody talked about it for a long time." The old woman passed away some twenty years ago and, being the good grandson, Jaromir went to help clear out her house.

He found the charred gloves in a box. By then he was well aware of Jiri Kolouch's labors at the site and the fact that, by then, many mementos had been moved from Jiri's house to a small city museum. Jaromir made the link to Miss Fortune and decided they must have belonged to the lone airman who survived the crash, Ray Noury. Jiri agreed that the gloves could be important, and that they might indeed have belonged to Ray. Such gloves were typically worn on a B-24 by waist gunners standing at their .50-calibers, the icy air rushing in as they struggled to fight off German attacks through the open window.

In a small, private moment during the 2004 commemoration Jaromir handed "Ray's gloves" to Ray himself. "He was very moved," Jaromir recounts. "Ray was totally surprised. He hugged me. I was happy, he was happy, everybody was happy. No, my life did not change. But I was pleased to give this man the important gift I could give."

If I thought my trip to Nepomuk would provide some sort of pop-psychology sense of "closure," I was wrong. Visiting the crash site, town, monuments and people brought nothing to conclusion. Instead, it opened my eyes. I learned about symbols of gratitude.

Some were the size of a museum; some were the size of a cross; some were the size of a glove; and some were the size of a tear. I saw an eagerness to recall, explain and record. I saw that, in Nepomuk, the past does not really live in the past. It is nearby, it is everywhere, and it is part of the present. That sense of past meeting present made the larger story of Miss Fortune's crew seem all the more immediate and all the more worthy of retelling. I still wanted to know the things my father refused to discuss. But that had become a goal, not the goal.

WEDDING PORTRAIT OF GRACE MALLOY AND JOE ALTEMUS, AUGUST 30, 1943.

CHAPTER TWELVE

"WE'RE GOING TO BE MARRIED"

When I began my search to understand my father's experience in World War II, Grace Altemus's letter incorporating Ray's still-fresh narration of Miss Fortune's final moments sent me on a longer journey than I had expected. As I learned more about everyone who had been touched by the tragedy, I saw that Miss Fortune's last mission and Grace's letter had melded ten grieving American families into one. That bond, I understood, lasted only for a time as new spouses, new homes, new children and new lives forced the tragedy on Dubec Hill slowly into memory. But, thanks to Grace, they all had been a family when they needed to be.

One more link intrigued me every bit as much, perhaps more: an unsigned, typed letter to Wayne's mother, "Mrs. Nelson," that spoke of the writer's overnight train trip to visit my father in the hospital outside Cleveland, returning just in time for work at Bethlehem Steel. It seemed like a letter from Grace in terms of writing style and appearance, not to mention the persuasive Bethlehem

BILL BOYCE AND GRACE ALTEMUS HODGSON AT HER HOME IN FLORIDA IN 2014.

connection, but as a lawyer, I wanted to know for sure. In the summer of 2014, as research on Miss Fortune's last mission began to connect all the pieces of the story for me, John Torrison told me he knew where Grace lived in Cocoa Beach. She was ninety-four and had been having health issues since the death of her second husband, Buddy. I determined I had to travel from Houston to Cocoa Beach to visit Grace.

Cocoa Beach is a quirky, only-in-America kind of place. Now primarily dependent on beach and cruise tourism, it was born as a residential area to support the space program centered at nearby Cape Canaveral. From the earliest Mercury flights through the moon landing in 1969 and the heyday of the space shuttle, Cape Canaveral (also known as Cape Kennedy after JFK's assassination) was the place to live for those enthralled by or involved in America's conquest of space. As Chris Hodgson, Grace's son who was there to help her after hip surgery, pointed out with delight, Larry Hagman's astronaut character on the popular '60s TV sitcom *I Dream of Jeanie* discovered the bottle containing Barbara Eden right near Grace's house.

The simple, one-story home was built on fingers of land created by dredging the Banana River. When the family arrived in 1965 after Buddy Hodgson retired from the Army, it was one of only two houses in the development. For most of the time the boys were growing up, the family had a boat—a twenty-six-foot, single-hull Grady White with outriggers for deep-sea fishing—docked just outside the back door.

Grace was wheelchair-bound when we met, though all indications were that she would walk again. The hip surgery took its toll, but after Chris—who has a restaurant background—moved up from Miami Beach and started cooking for her, she gained back some of the weight she'd lost and started on the road to recovery. She was scheduled after our visit to begin physical therapy aimed at getting her out of the wheelchair, making her more self-sufficient. "Now don't you dare," she giggled, "tell everybody I'm going into rehab!"

Meeting Grace was an extraordinary experience, a remarkable connection. Just as Skipper Miller is the only child born to any member of the Miss Fortune crew who died on Dubec Hill, Grace is the only surviving spouse. And yet, in a sense that took a while to settle in for me, she seemed less connected to the men who perished than many of the people I had come to know on my exploration. We all continued to feel the impact of February 22, regardless of whether we knew all the details. Unlike those of us who came to the scene years or even decades later, Grace had mourned Joe Altemus and moved on to live another life. In fact, at one point in her living room, she let on that she did not save the letters Joe Altemus wrote to her from overseas once she set a date with Buddy. "I was marrying another man," she explained.

Looking at her in her wheelchair, determined to eat and get to physical therapy at ninety-four, I understood that this is what the living must do for the dead, no matter how much we loved them. Because we loved them. Because we were loved in return.

I tuned back into what she was saying. "I remember Joe calling me and saying I needed to get our parents, his and mine, from Bethlehem to Langley Field in Virginia in one week," Grace was remembering. "George and Evelyn Goddard were there for our wedding. It was only about a month later that Evelyn drove me and Joe to the airfield. 'Now don't cry,' Joe told me. I think that was the last thing he ever said to me. Then I watched him walk away from me, across the tarmac. I know that's the last time I ever saw him."

So many years later, Grace doesn't think in long, involved stories about her brief time with Joe. She's more likely to share such stories about Buddy, the man who loved her and lived with her for fifty-plus years. In this conversation over a couple of hours and a lunch prepared by son Chris, there is a mention of Skipper here, an anecdote about Ray there. And then, when Grace's mind is ready, the brief memories come through loud and clear. On Joe charting the crew from the United States to Europe: "So there's my little navigator, who'd only been to high school—and he was the one who had to get them there." On George Goddard and what she's certain he went through in the crew's final moments: "He was trying so hard to get our boys back to Italy." And finally, on how it felt to receive Ray's letter and know in her heart she had to share it: "Some of the mothers were elderly, and definitely some of the grandmothers were elderly. It became my passion."

By the time Germany surrendered in May 1945, Joe and the rest of the crew had been moved from "missing in action" to "presumed dead" in the eyes of the government. The crew families all knew about Ray, understood he had survived the crash and lived out the war in German POW camps. They had a general understanding that he was allowed to write letters from wherever he was, mostly assurances he was being treated well that would pass the eyes of the camp censors. It was only as the war's ashes settled and its records were gathered that Grace heard the first details of her young husband's death on Dubec Hill, his remains gathered with all those from the crew and buried together in the faraway village of Pradlo.

CREW REBURIAL AT JEFFERSON BARRACKS NATIONAL CEMETERY IN 1950.

At some point she was notified that the U.S. Army had moved the combined remains to a military cemetery in France, and then in 1950 to Jefferson Barracks National Cemetery near St. Louis. There were many good reasons Grace did not travel to either of those brief, solemn ceremonies. By 1949, one was more important than all the rest.

Buddy Hodgson had served his country too—though he, like my father and so many others, refused to talk about it. Grace asked him what it was like, more than once: landing in Normandy on D-Day, later fighting off the German counterattack in the Ardennes Forest in Belgium, in the legendary Battle of the Bulge. As best she can recall, Buddy was willing or able to share nothing, except that on D-Day, he "wasn't in the first wave." He had fought bravely, though, as part of the U.S. Cavalry, which by 1944 meant tanks. There were dozens of important tank battles, and thousands of tank casualties, between D-Day and the end of the war, but Buddy survived these battles.

After their marriage, Grace and Buddy lived the Army life in the postwar era, being sent first to Greece as newlyweds in the bitter aftermath of that country's civil war. "It was my first time in a plane," Grace recalls. "And it wasn't a comfortable plane like the ones everybody flies around in today, I'll tell you that." By 1965, she became convinced that their sons would be healthiest in the sunshine and fresh air of the Florida coast. She persuaded Buddy to retire from the military and go to work with contractors helping the space program, companies like TWA and Boeing, which meant a new life in Cocoa Beach. Sitting today in her living room, Grace gives no indication she regrets any part of that decision. Chris ended up in Miami Beach and Key West, while Reggie and Peter are in the surfing business in Hawaii. None moved far from blue water—and neither has she.

Buddy eventually retired from all of his careers and, soon after, noticed the first signs of Alzheimer's. His final years were difficult but loving. As she described them, I remembered the emails she and John Torrison had shared. They often described trips to one doctor for her husband and another for their dog. Grace made many of these trips in the baby blue 1957 Thunderbird that still sat in her garage.

Buddy died in 2007 at the age of ninety-three. His ashes were stored at a local funeral home, awaiting Grace's when that day comes. "That's what we talked about and decided," she said. A smile sneaked onto her lips. "I guess he didn't know I'd make him wait this long."

Grace says it was "twenty-five years" after the war but it was substantially more than that when a letter arrived in the mail from the 98th Bomb Group, inviting her to attend a reunion. No doubt using the Internet, someone had traced Grace Hodgson back to Joe Altemus. "I called the man right away," Grace recounted. "And

I told him no, I wouldn't be interested in any reunion because I wouldn't know anybody there. But I would appreciate any information he might have about February 22, 1944. And he said, you know, there's another person asking us about that very same day."

That other person was John Torrison. John, that dogged web researcher with an uncle lost in the crash before he was born, met Grace, fast, accurate typist, crew widow and all-round lively human being. Theirs was an email pen-pal relationship made in heaven, across generations, connecting the families once again. As I had discovered, the two wrote often and in detail. Through John, Grace kept up with Ray's final years, including his two visits to the anniversary commemorations in Nepomuk, the development of the crash-site memorial and the creation of the town museum. By this time, Buddy's Alzheimer's had grown so severe that Grace was in no position to travel across an ocean, even had she felt the least bit comfortable about doing so.

Finally, after we had enjoyed our lunch, perused old photos and exchanged favorite stories, it was time to say goodbye. There were more stories, surely, more moments that could be revisited with enough time and enough space. Yes, Grace did visit my father in Cleveland. Yes, she did take an overnight train from Bethlehem, getting back just in time for work at Bethlehem Steel. "Good girls didn't do such things in those days," Grace said, flashing a conspiratorial grin. "But I did." And yes, she had heard about my father from Joe and later about where he was recovering from Ray. Yet if she traveled hoping for more information about her missing husband—more tidbits to keep hope alive via the combat grapevine—she was disappointed. "Really," Grace recalled matter-of-factly of her meeting with my father, "we had nothing to say."

Having explored her connection to my father, I understood that it was time to go home. Back to Houston. Back to court. Most of all, back to Maria, and back to my own children. Yet even as I recognized this, Grace recognized something different. Without warning, she embarked on her longest, most detailed story of our visit.

"I only had one date with Joe," she announced, gazing out from her wheelchair. I had stood to leave and now returned to the seat beside her. "Before we got married, I mean. You know, I was just your small-town snob back them." She laughs. "Even though we both worked at Bethlehem Steel, Joe lived on the South Side. I had no desire to go out with him. None. I think he probably liked me already, but we never did anything about it, and probably never would have except for the war. Joe went off to California for training and, when he came back, he walked into our office—tanned, with blond curly hair, built beautifully, and wearing that uniform like nobody ever did. We both stopped. We could have been married right there."

Grace stopped, remembering their first and only date, and especially the way it ended. Her voice is softer than it has been. Her gaze was clearer, more intense. "We got back in his car. And he kissed me and said 'We're going to be married.' All I said was, 'I know.'" However much life she had lived since that night, Joe Altemus' first date with his only bride still lived on, a memory to be shared with others.

Since the moment when I acted on the impulse to call Ray in March 2013, I had come to know so many stories, all linked to mine. I had learned stories of those who lived long, imperfect lives and stories of others who weren't given that chance, learned stories of those who loved each other for decades and of those who shared only a moment. For me, all these stories began far from my home, on a hillside where on a snowy, dreary winter's day a plane fell out of the sky, and concluded with the understanding I found in Cocoa Beach, having lunch with an elderly lady whose name I hadn't known eighteen months earlier.

Grace had done the best she could, as a young woman saying "I know" to that young navigator, just as she'd do later as a young widow, retyping the words of a surviving airman she had never met. In those acts, Grace did what we all are called to do—believing, hoping, loving. For me, Grace was both giver and gift, and at that point, I thought my search for my father had come to a peaceful conclusion. The past, however, had more to reveal.

CREW PHOTOGRAPH TAKEN ON FEBRUARY 15, 1944, L TO R: RAY NOURY,
WAYNE NELSON, HAROLD CARTER, MEL ADAMS, ROY HUGHES.

CHAPTER THIRTEEN

WATER IN
THE DESERT

had not expected to find quite so many letters. And the more I found, the harder I looked. I felt compelled to search out words and people who could help me approximate the conversation I never had with my father. John Torrison had collected the names and contact information of survivors and relatives—sometimes distant—for each of the crew members. We wrote to all of them. Some responded; some did not. Some had information or letters; some did not. Some wanted to talk; some did not. I already had learned more from Ray, John, Grace, Skipper, Mary Hevener and the people of Nepomuk than I had dared to imagine. Still, I was anxious to meet with anyone else who could open a door to 1944.

And so I was thrilled when I received a note in the mailbox with a return address in Lubbock, Texas containing precise handwriting that began, "Dear Bill Boyce." The note came from Wanda Sikes, the sister of top turret gunner Roy Hughes. Wanda wrote: "I am glad to receive your note and also to contribute any way I can with the story of our crew." I soon was on my way to Lubbock.

Roy Hughes was less than a month short of his twenty-third birthday when Miss Fortune was shot down in 1944. The telegram that declared him missing arrived in Friona, Texas, on his actual birthday, March 17. His mother received it in her hospital bed, two days after surgery for the cancer she'd never had a chance to write him about. Written a few days later, that letter came back to her as undeliverable. Roy's younger sister Wanda remembered the sight of their mother in that bed, the government telegram read, her face turned against the wall.

Shortly before Labor Day in 2014, I went to visit with Wanda Sikes in the comfortable Lubbock, Texas, senior-living apartment she shares with her husband, a retired U.S. naval officer. Wanda had spent the previous few weeks going through letters and photographs in preparation for my visit. Looking at old photos of Roy around the house in Friona, and finally posing with Miss Fortune's crew, she's made a remarkable discovery about her brother. "I can't have a good memory of him unless I'm looking at pictures," she said. "So I sometimes can't remember if I'm just remembering the pictures."

FAMILY PHOTO OF WANDA, ROY, LUCY MAE, AND BUFORD HUGHES IN FRIONA, TEXAS.

Like virtually everyone John Torrison and I met on this journey, Wanda had never forgotten her brother—the way he always seemed picked on by the three older girls, the way he was nice to her, the way he was seldom seen around their house on the edge of Friona without his dog known only as "Pooch" or "Hound" because "we never really got around to naming him." But she hadn't thought about Roy directly, not this much and certainly not this directly, in decades. "We were grieving and hoping," she recalled of the year or two that began with the telegram. "But after a while you have your own families. You have to."

In a small office with a desk piled high with letters held in groups by rubber bands, many bearing Post-It Notes about why she thought a particular letter might be interesting, and an underlying thatch of news clippings and black-and white photos, Wanda started telling Roy's story. By the time we finished talking, she also had revealed another significant piece of my father's story.

In our initial phone conversations, Wanda told me how blessed she felt to have something to show at all. The box that contained Roy's World War II memorabilia seemed to be missing after the couple had moved into the facility. "Our kids said 'Go,'" she explains, and that was all there was to that. Two different people did the packing up of their house, and then, in the new place, there was no box. Eventually, though, it turned up, and Wanda felt it was divine intervention that kept these memories around long enough for our visit. There had been other things from Roy and the war, possibly pieces from the crash site and other things. "But we had to let them go," Wanda says.

Not all the memories brought on by this exercise were sad. She remembered Friona, her mother caring for the children around the house, her father working for parts of her childhood in the oilfields and at a gas station. She remembered her mother hanging wet sheets on all the windows whenever the dust storms that marked the 1930s came and she remembered the long, hard recovery from the Great Depression. "Maybe it got better in the North and the East," she says, "because up there they had industry. It was still pretty hard down here."

They were desperate times in more ways than one. It was the age of Bonnie and Clyde and other gangsters who captured the public imagination, at least partly for their rebellion against the moral, legal and financial system that had failed America so profoundly. When he was sixteen, Roy himself was kidnapped, lured into a car by criminals who mistook him for the richest kid in town. They realized their mistake about five miles out of Friona on the road to Clovis, New Mexico and released the young man to walk back home in the dark. Roy told his mother what had happened, and she was rightly horrified. Perhaps she'd never quite pondered how easy it was for somebody to take Roy from her forever.

By the time the war loomed, the Hughes family's only son— virtually all of Roy's letters to his mother would be signed "Your Favorite Son"—wanted the two things many young men of that time wanted. He wanted to serve his country in defeating its many enemies, and he wanted to avoid the infantry. He had picked up a love for flying hanging around with the family that owned Friona's small airport, and he set out to be a Navy pilot. There he was sorely disappointed. An examining doctor noticed a scar near his ribs caused by a tube used to treat childhood pneumonia and turned him away. "In those days pneumonia was a death sentence," Wanda explained "The doctor told Roy, 'You should be dead.'"

Fearing a repeat but trying to keep his hopes alive, Roy applied for the Army Air Corps. This time no one noticed, or perhaps no one cared, that he "should" have died when he was three. Long before he met up with the men of Miss Fortune, Roy Hughes started training as a gunner for one of the Army Air Corps' big bombers that would play a major role in the destruction of Hitler's ability to wage war. By late April 1943, he was in Harlingen, where the Gulf of Mexico meets the Texas-Mexico border.

"Boy," Roy wrote home, "these dang guns and stuff is complicated as hell, with a million parts to learn the name of and what they do. We also have three different kinds of power turrets to learn to operate and what makes them tick. Ok! gosh I hate to think of what I've got to do to pass this dang course." Left unsaid was the fact that the infantry scooped up many soldiers who failed such courses.

Roy passed, writing home several times to share his scores, espe-cially when it came to shooting the "skeet"—clay pigeons moving at sixty-five miles an hour, he explained for the folks back home. "Boy, I'm getting to be a dead eye dick," he reported.

For all the distance, Friona and his old life never left Roy Hughes entirely. At one point, presumably once he'd been shipped over-seas and assigned to Miss Fortune's crew, he reported to his mother on problems with his former girlfriend, a young woman named Wynona. She wasn't answering his letters and seemed to be drift-ing away, beyond his romantic reach. A "Dear Roy" letter seemed to be looming.

"A lot of the girls were getting desperate," Wanda told me. She had been too young at the time to worry but old enough to notice. "All their boys were going off to war and getting killed. Some of the girls married whoever was still around." With all Roy had to learn and do to stay alive, reading his letters, I had the feeling that such issues had begun to fade like so many "things of a child" that GIs had been forced to put away. "Don't let it worry you," Roy reassured his mother, "because it sure don't bother me. I haven't time to worry about women, this is a full time job over here."

On January 24, 1944, less than a month before his plane would go down, Roy wrote home about his special bond with Miss Fortune's crew. As family members would discover in the months and years after the crash, it was a bond that would transcend the loss and even the violence of the crew's death. "Yes, we are all still together except one," he wrote. "Boyce isn't with us anymore. All our officers are still with us… and believe me, they are all the best guys in the whole damn world."

On February 14, he wrote again, directly responding to his mother's long string of letters filled with Christian encouragement, with the simple faith that leaving our lives and fates and futures in God's hands was the only way to respond to this terrible war. In the ungilded eloquence of Roy's response, it's clear he was getting the message. "Yes mother I read my pocket Bible a lot," he wrote. "I even have a copy of the 93rd Psalm pasted in my turret on the plane." In the King James version, that passage would have assured him, "The Lord on high is mightier than the noise of many waters, yea, than the mighty waves of the sea." "There is more praying done in any bomber," Roy concluded, "than in any church—and we all have faith and trust."

Roy's mother continued to write to him long past February 22, 1944, because his fate wasn't known, confirmed or even officially presumed for many months. World War II mothers were known to hold onto their belief their sons could walk through the door at any minute, some keeping the faith in a return even for decades. There was always Switzerland, which might have harbored the crew in some way long after the crash. There were always Resistance fighters, long after there was a war to fight, still hiding in some remote mountain pass. And of course, there was always amnesia. Every time a veteran turned up—even one—not remembering who he was or where he belonged, it provided new hope and ultimately new pain for thousands of mothers whose sons would never turn up.

One of Mrs. Hughes' most poignant letters to Roy remains the one she wrote explaining her cancer. She lived barely two more years. Her timeless mother's wish, written days before her son's death but returned to her unreceived, reads: "Don't worry about me. I am going to be good as new. You first take care of yourself and write often, and hurry home. I love you always my soldier son. Mom."

In the mix of letters in Wanda's possession was one to all the crew families sent by Evelyn Goddard on May 22, 1944. It is mostly a letter sent to her from Melvin Adams, who continued to fly with another crew after missing the February 22 mission to Regensburg. By this point, I recognized the format: a letter than is, almost entirely, a retyped letter from someone else.

A brief handwritten note at the bottom was Evelyn's effort to be supportive, to be courageous—"Dearest Mom, how's this for good news." That was the clear intent of Mel's letter. "I have a feeling that George landed in some field," Mel says to George's wife, "and there are rumors that the boys aren't far off. As you know, and Boyce and I do, George and Kandy are two pilots that would bring that ship and crew through if there was the least possible chance... Evelyn, I would rest in ease and keep believing all are fine."

In a one-liner that suggests what research later supported, Mel said that Miss Fortune was shot down "on the way up," which offered clues about its route through what he called the "Skunks territory," presumably a Nazi-occupied place like Czechoslovakia. And while expressing joy that my father was recovering so well at the hospital in Cleveland, Mel also served up a rare and remarkably honest glimpse of how he felt at the end of that terrible day. "I believe that was the first time the crew flew without me," Mel writes, "and when the planes came back, I went out to see them, but one of our aircraft was missing. I could barely keep from bawling when the fellows told me the news. I came straight back to the barracks and bawled for half the night."

I later asked Mel Adams's son, Melvin A. Adams Jr., about this letter and his father's willingness to discuss Miss Fortune's crew. "He couldn't talk about it, ever," said his son. "Anything I knew I heard from my mother, and she didn't say too much because she knew he didn't want to talk about it." I figured Mel Adams Jr. had spent time at the kitchen table with a Do Not Ask List that looked a lot like mine.

"He was the crew chief, and he thought he should have been on the plane that day to take care of things," his son explained. "But he was grounded at the last minute, and the plane didn't come back. He came close to having a breakdown after the plane was shot down."

Mel Adams Sr. went on to serve in the Army, and later the Air Force, for a dozen years. He went to Korea before leaving the service in the mid-1950s to begin his post-military life as a mechanic and, eventually, the owner of a carpet-cleaning company in New Jersey. He had his own heroic moments, including one instance in which he saved his plane as it attempted to land by kicking loose a bomb that was stuck in the rack. And yet, until his death in 1998, Mel Adams could not get past and could not discuss the mission he had missed in February 1944. Said his son: "Dad just would not talk."

Another letter to Mrs. Hughes came from Lou Belle Spickard, the bombardier's mother. The message one grieving crew mother sent to another is both simple and profound. Mom Spickard's letter to Mom Hughes starts with this caption: "Copy of Son's farewell letter to me—minus very personal paragraphs—dated February 9, 1944, and which I found in his Bible, next to the 23rd Psalm, his favorite, when his belongings came back from Italy in July, 1944."

Charles Spickard's February 9 letter to his mother contains no cheery assurances that all is well in Italy, no promises of an eventual homecoming. Time was short, the situation was desperate, and luck was a fragile shield. Charles aimed his words with a bombardier's precision. "I've been wanting to write this letter for some time, and now seems like the time to do it. After a lay off of a month we are back to flying missions again. From the looks of things we will all be pretty lucky if we get through all our missions."

After thanking his mother for teaching him "so many invaluable things...such as sportsmanship, a faith in God and the future, clean living, and so many things I've done my best to live up to all these years," Charles got to the heart of the matter. "Now for the other thing: If I should get mine while I am up there in the clouds, I want you to know that I'm not afraid of going. Of course I want so much to get back to you, and to start a home of my own. That's really all that I'm living for right now. If I do go though I'm ready for it."

Charles continued, "When I go I feel sure that I'll be under God's care and maybe with my Jim...before too long." Lou Belle explained in an aside to Mom Hughes that Jim was Charles's "first buddy who was killed on a training flight Christmas eve, 1942." Charles went on: "I've always tried to live the sort of life that God likes, and even though I've gone astray a few times I feel certain that I shall be forgiven."

Charles closed his farewell letter with these thoughts: "I hope when you read this that you won't be feeling too badly." He continues, "Of course I know it will hurt you deeply. Remember though that God knows best and have faith in Him for He is right. Then too have faith that someday we will be together again in a land where there are no troubles and cares."

The shadows grew longer in the small office as afternoon progressed and Wanda wound down her narration of her family's wartime life. She cried a number of times at specific memories of her brother, but laughed even more, smiling at so much that was good. She looked up from her stacks of letters and said, "We've had this one here for a long time. I think it's time for you to take it with you."

I had promised to faithfully return a few earlier items she had offered to share, and I didn't understand at first. Wanda emphasized, "No, Bill, I think this one needs to go home with you." She handed me the envelope, and I recognized the handwriting on it as though it were my own.

Postmarked Cleveland, Ohio, dated May 10, 1944, and bearing the return address Crile General Hospital, the letter begins with the salutation "Dear Mom Hughes." My father had written it as soon as he could get up from bed after having yet another cast removed. In this letter, he applauded the heartening news about the crew, especially that contained in the recent letter from Mel Adams. And he reiterated the hope that constituted the very air that all waiting families breathed through this period, that there were parachutes spotted among the clouds, that "the big boy upstairs" was lovingly in charge, and that Adams clearly was trying to communicate more good news than he was allowed to by the censors.

"I also have," he wrote, "as you say, a lot of feeling for Melvin. I know what it was, and is, to him to be carrying on, with another crew, when he was, is, so deeply attached to our crew. I shall write him soon, in hopes that he may relay some interesting information to us, and to also wish him the best of luck. He is a grand fellow."

I was breathless as I read the rest of my father's letter. I was not sure what I actually expected or wanted to read. He wrote of "The Boys," and specifically of Mrs. Hughes' only and "favorite son."

"Roy was considered the best of the crew," he told her. "He was tops." This was true not least, he offered, because of Roy's dreams for all he would do once this war had been won. "He loved his native land," my father wrote, "and he could do wonders for it. Boyce—he would say—get water to that so-called desert and she'll grow anything you want."

There was much gratitude in this special letter, thanking her for the "swell" portrait of Roy that I had discovered in my father's papers. My father also thanked her for the "swell" news clipping about Roy's military service from the Friona paper. There was the promise that a Mother's Day card is on the way. "It's from Roy," he wrote with the gentlest wink, "by me."

Finally, in a passage that will forever assure me that the time I had taken from my own family to explore the past had been worth the effort, there is a moment of such hope, such humility, such faith and such unintentional eloquence that I offer it to anyone who travels in search of a departed parent—and, therefore, in search of self.

"My helping you is, I think, very limited," wrote my father, Staff Sgt. William D. Boyce, before the many operations on his leg, before his honorable discharge from the Army, before his marriage, before what I had always assumed was his real life. "But it is good to be able to write to you, + all the parents of the fellows, as you say. I was so close too. It is as if we were coming home one at a time, + I happened to be the first + I am just writing to fill in while the others return."

If Grace had given me peace, Wanda provided perspective. Was there anything that remained for me to learn from Miss Fortune?

CREW MEMORIAL AT DUBEC HILL CRASH SITE IN 2009.

CHAPTER FOURTEEN

THE CHASM
OF WORDS

At the Czech Center of Houston in a room longer than it was wide, with windows along one side and books going back to the mid-1800s on all the other walls, I sat with Marie Mann, a Czech-English translator, and dug through books, articles and her English translations of them, crossing the chasm of time, of distance and, most of all at this meeting, of the Czech language. I hoped she would be able to answer some questions and solve some lingering mysteries about February 22, 1944. Chief among these questions was this one: If Miss Fortune was on a mission to bomb Regensburg, why did its last flight end some 150 kilometers away away on a Czech hillside?

But I was disappointed.

"The translation," she says, "is not very good sometimes." I wasn't sure if she was being modest. She mentioned, "There is the letter Ray Noury wrote in English," and I explained I knew Ray's letter quite well. "In the book, much of the letter is translated into Czech. And some parts are not well done." In other words, if I thought fluency in Czech and a pile of books and documents would bring the image of Miss Fortune and its crew into perfect focus, I was mistaken. Marie was a retired chemist from Shell, in the industrial Houston area called Deer Park, and she knew an inexact science when she saw one. Translation, we stand cautioned, unlike chemistry, is an extremely inexact science.

I had acquired some odds and ends, including documents given to the Torrisons and me during visits to Nepomuk, Pradlo and the crash site on Dubec Hill. Plus, Marie had taken the initiative to find various online essays and reports, some in Czech needing her translation and others already in English, about the air war in Europe in general and the fights over her native land in particular. Within months of our visit, she planned to make a trip home. "If you would like me to go to this place and check out something," she said, "it is okay. I can do it."

The big assignment before her was Karel Foud's self-published book in Czech titled *Operace Argument*—"Operation Argument" in English. Few flyers then realized—Goddard's crew surely among them—how important the Operation Argument sorties that became Big Week would be, training the air power of all the Allies on cities with factories that kept the Luftwaffe flying. This was hardly the first effort to cripple the German air machine, but this was total, this was concentrated, this was big. Only a handful of people on earth knew the assault's true purpose: to ground the Luftwaffe's bombers and fighter planes in order to give the Allies a fighting chance on those Normandy beaches only five months later. And to make Fortress Europe crumble, starting on D-Day.

Month after month, I had interviewed people and consulted books on all aspects of the European air war. Those efforts had felt like research. Something about staring at pages printed in Czech and then perusing Marie's rendering into English made it feel like eavesdropping. It made what I was learning seem excitingly true.

"This event kept the Nepomuk region excited for a long time," I read in the book's preface, in Marie's English, "and even was talked about in nearby Plzen. It was kept in the subconscious of the local residents after the end of all war hardship. Not even the post February communistic regime, whose officials tried with all the effort"—the sentence tangles badly here, but in some ways it was the clearest statement I had heard—"suppressed the role of the American army and all the other western allies in the liberation of the republic and even concentrated Soviet oriented propaganda did not erased the memory of the American pilots fall on Dubci from the mind of the population. Contrary, the role of the Americans in the liberation of the Western Czech was gaining an element of 'forbidden fruit' and the acts which were held at few memorials (monuments) dedicated to fallen American soldiers become in the mind of many symbols of resentment against the regime."

Throughout the months of inquiring—and of course the years of research done by John Torrison in the States, along with the various Czech excavations on Dubec Hill—we had not arrived at a clear explanation of why Miss Fortune's last mission ended where it did. Yes, the target was Regensburg. But did the planes fly over the Nepomuk region on the way to Regensburg, since they crashed around noon before a projected bombing time of 1 p.m.? Did they, as some accounts suggested, make it to Regensburg, drop or not drop their bombs, and then fly or get chased over the Czech Protectorate? Or, as a couple of written records hint with ambiguity, did they reach Regensburg, decide conditions were too cloudy for a bombing run and then choose the legendary "Skoda Works" in Plzen (where Skoda cars are made in the Czech Republic to this day) as an alternative target? Bomber pilots were under pressure to make something of their flights, whether it was bombing their primary target or something else.

The book's discussion of Mission #189—the number of bombing attacks launched by the 98th Bomb Group and "all ready the third day of night and day attacks against German plane manufacturing factories"—stops short of addressing the questions that remain about Miss Fortune's last mission. But by quoting the "day order" given pilots and navigators that early morning, *Operace Argument* brought me closer to the moment Ray talked about in his letter when he shared Goddard's announcement that the mission would be to Regensburg and they could "expect the worst."

Citing a version of an apparently lost military record, translated from English to Czech and then back again, *Operace Argument* outlines the mission. "Intelligence department is not given any concrete information about the number of light and heavy anti craft machine guns in Regensburg," we read. "On the way to Regensburg, our formation will go through the operation zone of enemies and chase fighters from the base in Mostar, Zagreb, Klagenfurt, Styrsky Hradec and the vicinity of Vienna." As those places are today in Bosnia, Croatia and Austria (indeed, Styrsky Hradec is now called Graz), the slightest change in their sequence would make for an entirely different flight path—not to mention an entirely different answer to the question about Regensburg.

The day order includes an evaluation of the enemy's readiness to keep the bombers away, estimating there were 75-100 fighter planes (specifically Me109s and Ju88s), all furnished with rockets. Mostar and Zagreb were considered fairly safe, but all the rest—deadly. The Luftwaffe along the route was capable of carrying out "40-50 protection starts." Still, says the order, the likely sacrifice will be worth it. "The given target has the highest priority," it declares, "because here is produced a large number of Me109s. It is estimated that by destroying the given target the enemy will lose production for nine months." In other words, two thousand Messerschmitts for killing Allied troops would never be built.

The book quoted from a speech given that morning by the commanding officer. This too, even in English-Czech-English, pointed to a likely flight path: "Lecce to Mesagne," where planes from the 98th would meet up with counterparts from the 449th, then "Bitondo, Volkermarkt, Waidhofen to the initiation point." Forming a V, the bombers would eventually fly over Regensburg and release their payloads from around twenty-three thousand feet. Suddenly, thinking of that altitude in terms of commercial air travel, the idea of a thick cloud cover makes sense. The planes would be a long way up, with plenty of room for cloud bank to conspire with cloud bank and virtually wipe out all vision of the city far below. "The target," this officer is quoted as saying, "will be given by leader of the mission and all others will dump the bombs accordingly."

So, such a leader could choose to redirect the attack from Regensburg to Plzen if conditions seemed to merit. He certainly had what one history of the period calls "carte blanche." But if he had done so, why is "Regensburg" the only place ever mentioned in the records? The Skoda Works in Plzen would have been a feather in any bomb group's cap.

Though the writing and translation got murky, a picture slowly emerged. Goddard's plane took off from Italy about 8 a.m., with nineteen other Liberators and "two planes extra." Within a fairly short time, however, no fewer than seven bombers dropped out of formation and returned to various U.S. bases because of breakdowns. Some engines weren't working properly, sending a clear message to scrap a mission that would require flying over the Alps and, potentially, over hundreds of miles of enemy territory. Another Liberator turned back because "there was not enough oxygen." And all the while as the formation from the 98th was thinning out, so was the 449th, the group they were supposed to meet.

The record suggests the gathered bombers made it to Regensburg—this may have meant all did or only some. It took 120 seconds to zero in on the target, we are told, and the bombs were dropped accordingly. One in-the-moment report from the group said "the results of the bombing were not possible to observe because the weather above the target was 10/10 overcast" (meaning completely obscured). The preliminary report stated that "bombs probably reached the target."

Various planes dropped payloads between 12:45 and 1:12 p.m. By then, according to some eyewitness accounts, Miss Fortune had already crashed into Dubec Hill about 150 kilometers away.

It must be some kind of fool's errand, across a distance of seventy years, with at least that many German fighters in the sky above Czechoslovakia that day, to attempt determine exactly who shot down Miss Fortune. Yet that was what I was hoping to do as Marie Mann translated these documents. A few originally were written in German, discovered later in the archives of the Third Reich. But nearly all had been filtered over the decades through the research of Czechs looking into what happened. As best I can tell, there is no official or final determination by either side of which pilot gets credit for the "kill."

There have been enticing rumors, as animosity from the war faded, of an aging German pilot who talked of shooting down Miss

Fortune at various reunions. These were typically warm-hearted affairs, especially for airmen. These soldiers always stood out from all others for the special way they viewed the guy or guys in the other plane. Such men were not the "enemy," they would stress to anyone willing to listen, but only the "opponent." Flying missions was a sport, a noble competition, to such men, and you get the feeling they hoped winners could be chosen without anyone having to die. There is at least one story of a fighter pilot who, defying orders from above, helped a crippled opponent make his way back to safety. Of course, it was all-out war, and many, many airmen did die. But it's worth pondering these differences.

From a distance of too much time, in Marie's translations, two German fighter pilots captured my attention. Neither lived to see the end of the war, the first dying later the same day that Miss Fortune fell on Dubec Hill.

The first is Friedrich Muer. In his photograph, he looks as though he might be fourteen. He is boyish in every way, appearing to not even need to shave. Innocent good looks shine from beneath the pilot's cap whose brim obscures his light eyebrows. A memorandum from the Luftwaffe high command names him as the pilot who, on February 22, 1944, shot down a B-24 Liberator. There were, we now know, two other Liberators downed in the same area at about the same time. Muer, flying out of the airbase called Lestiste Wels in Austria, may, in the end, have shot down any one of them, not necessarily Miss Fortune. Obviously, the battle continued later into the day. During one of his encounters, Muer's Messerschmitt was shot down, killing him. All we have is the portrait of this near-child who was handed the power to deliver quick death.

If Hollywood were casting Goddard's adversary, it would without hesitation choose the German ace named Egon Albrecht, the second pilot. In the sole photo of him, he exudes Nazi efficiency and discipline. His eyes gaze coldly somewhere away from the camera, his hair slicked back, his chin unyielding above the Iron Cross that hangs around his neck. Evidence suggests it may well have been Albrecht who bested Goddard's gunners.

Albrecht was born shortly before the end of World War I, not in Germany but of German parents in Brazil—the place many

escaping Nazis would reach after World War II. As the new con-
flagration neared, he made his way to Germany under obscure
circumstances and angled his way toward aviation. He was attracting attention with his flying as early as 1940 and, two years later,
played a legendary role in Germany's doomed invasion of Russia.
During that effort, known as Operation Barbarossa, he earned the
Knight's Cross for two-hundred-fifty military actions. His score—
as fighter pilots think of such things—was eleven downed enemy
planes, 162 destroyed cars, 243 horse carriages, three locomotives,
thirty cannons and eight bunkers. By 1943, he was flying missions
from the French coast, going up against a cadre of brave Czech
fighter pilots who by then were supporting their occupied country
by flying with the British RAF.

Albrecht's record earned him the role of unit leader—definitely
the role he played above the Nepomuk region on February 22.
From the gathered evidence, the linking of Albrecht to the Goddard
plane still seems more anecdotal than official, which makes the
imprecision of multi-language translation all the more frustrating.

Albrecht himself never got to confirm or deny it. Sent aloft by
a force decimated by Big Week, Albrecht did his best to defend the
Reich from its miles of Normandy invaders. He was flying a Bf-109
G-14W near Creil on August 25, 1944, when he was shot down and
killed. In the war records of the Third Reich, Albrecht is credited
with twenty-five victories in his career, including five four-engine
heavy bombers. One may have been Miss Fortune. Even this clue
seemed less significant than I once thought it would be. I had come
to care far less about the Luftwaffe ace who did the hunting than
I did about the airmen who did the dying.

Sitting on the third floor of the Czech Center in Houston, listening as Marie Mann read through page after page of her translations—sometimes verbatim, sometimes in loose summaries—I felt
painfully close to that B-24. With the next stack of printer papers,
I was transported to ground level in the villages surrounding Dubec.

As recounted in Karel Foud's book, an eyewitness known only
as "Mr. Karnan," described how part of Miss Fortune's right wing
was torn off "with the engine" and "in a while landed on Bukova
Hill between Blokovice and Nepomuk in Plzen region." That wing

and engine hit the ground first, in a place apart from the crash site and apart from where Ray Noury landed with his faulty parachute. "The trees supporting the wing were all burn out." The "spinning fuselage" (so the early eyewitnesses described it), with the whole left wing and the rest of the right, landed "vertically" in the small garden in the vicinity of the forest ranger's cottage on Dubec Hill.

In *Operace Argument,* Karel Foud includes a flourish of unrehearsed, sometimes confusing or contradictory accounts from villagers on the ground—not hard to understand when a large airplane had just fallen nearby. There were descriptions of the crash site, which quickly that afternoon became a place of immense curiosity; details of the fires kept going around the plane by high-octane fuel and exploding machine gun ammunition; a mention of the crater dug by the plane when it struck, fifteen meters long and three meters deep; descriptions of the plane pieces, those not obliterated by the various explosions, "deformed" by the intense heat. And as we had heard ourselves from survivors who were there, descriptions again about the body parts—the scattered limbs, the organs hanging from trees. No one who saw that gruesome sight would ever forget it. And then, there was Ray.

"Little after noon I heard the planes and run out on the backyard, from there," offered train dispatcher Frantisek Slajz from the village of Zhuri. "I observed six planes flying from Blokovic to Zdirec. Then I heard the shooting of machine guns and saw the wing from one of the planes falling to the ground and the fuselage flying to direction to village Pradlo. The fuselage was in flames. Between the falling wing and the burning fuselage I noticed the open parachute."

According to his account, Slajz was the first to reach Ray—he was the man Ray asked if he was German or Czech, with the answer coming as a relief. Slajz released him from the chute, helped him stand but then, noticing Ray was wounded, held a brief, makeshift conversation with him on a surprising array of topics. Ray, he said, was wearing three pairs of socks (against the extreme cold of flying) but no shoes. "There was hidden 10cm silver medallion with the black statue of Jesus in his sock," the Czech reported. "Under the cross was a silver plate with his name and date of birth. He took it and put it in his overall. He pointed out that he got it from his mother and that was his talisman."

A scene ensued after Slajz offered to carry Ray to safety. As soon as he started to lift, he noted others coming closer and feared they either were Germans or would turn him in, so he carried Ray into the trees to hide. The people saw this and followed, so Slajz took Ray back to the place he'd landed. The man concluded: "He was hugging and kissing me. After I put him on the original place there were people. They took care of him and I left."

Jan Keller of Chocenice, then a thirty-four-year-old cabinet-maker, was one of those people. "Some persons took him willingly and unhesitatingly and carried him away," Keller told police at the time. "Josef Hajsman took off his coat for the pilot (everyone figured Ray was the pilot) to be carried on comfortably. Keller followed the group, carrying Ray's bundled-up parachute. All the time we carried the pilot from the forest, a few American planes circled above us without interfering." There is nothing in the American record about planes "circling," and with seventy-plus German fighters searching for their next prey, this seems unlikely.

According to Keller, Ray was taken to the police station—and, as in all the accounts, warmed around a fire and bandaged as best the villagers could. A splinter pulled from Ray's leg became a valued souvenir: "I still have that splinter," Keller boasted at the time.

The drama of the German occupation comes through in an account added in 1946, this time by police Sgt. Zdenek Sima. Once Ray was delivered to the station in Chocenice, the tangled powers of the war came into the picture. "Helena Suchmanova, wife of chief sergeant, who lived in the station, brought a liquor for the pilot and he drank it," Sima said two years after the event. "Because all in the vicinity of Chocenice knew that the fallen pilot was at our station, I had to report the event to the district police station in Plzen, who informed Gestapo, which at the time resided in Blovice. Shortly afterward I got a call from German Hons from Blovice that the Gestapo recently drives from Plzen to Chocenice because of the pilot."

"At that moment Suchmanova entered again and wanted to give some kolaches to the pilot. I could not let it happen, because I knew that every minute the Gestapo can come. Immediately after her departure the Gestapo arrived at the station."

Ray's ordeal as a POW had begun.

It was hardly smooth sailing for Sima either. Even as the ruins of the plane smoldered on the hillside, the police sergeant was arrested by the Gestapo at the train station and put through a rigorous interrogation. "They took me to the baggage storage and asked me in German if I got any documents from the jumped pilot," Sima said, referring to Ray as the airman who jumped from the plane. "I pretended that I do not understand German and they slap me in the face. When I was not answering in German, they started speak Czech and I make sure that they knew I did not get any documents. They pretended the pilot was not American but German, and they wanted to know what I got from that German pilot. When they could not find anything from me, they let me go."

I feared there would be too little information left after seventy years to figure out what happened to Miss Fortune. I should have prepared instead for the challenge of finding too much information, some of which was confusing or contradictory.

As surely as I can determine, and perhaps as surely as anyone ever will, the B-24 Liberator named Miss Fortune piloted by George Goddard was shot down in the Nepomuk region of today's Czech Republic during a fierce attack by German fighters. It may have been shot down by Friedrich Muer, who perished later that day, or by famed ace Egan Albrecht, who was killed six months later. Only one of the eleven crewmen, Ray Noury, survived that day. Noury survived brutal treatment as a prisoner of war and lived into his ninth decade in Rhode Island; for many years, he never mentioned that any of these things had happened. Only in his old age did Ray start talking. His story became, for many, a bridge between present and past, and a memorial to a generation that had sacrificed so much and told others so little about it.

Miss Fortune's last mission was to bomb the Messerschmitt production factories in Regensburg. It never returned. Later, the bombing would be declared "successful" by the Allies and regarded as a significant part of Operation Argument or, more popularly, Big Week—the top-secret strategy to cripple the Luftwaffe in preparation for the even more top-secret D-Day invasion of Nazi-occupied France. The invasion would take its high-profile place in the history of warfare, but the crash of a B-24 on a wintry hill would be almost completely forgotten, except by those who cared for the men lost there.

Others kept the story alive too, including people who lived in an occupied, terrorized land under a government that tried everything it could to make them forget. They safeguarded and cherished this knowledge through the end of one totalitarian regime and the entire lifespan of another. The people who lived near Dubec Hill on February 22, 1944, never forgot, and even their children and grandchildren hold onto these events. The simple act of remembering, and nodding to others who remembered, became its own silent act of courage, of freedom, of defiance.

John Torrison and I, separately and together, undertook journeys to discover these facts. After meeting Ray, Skipper, Grace and Wanda, traveling to the crash site, sifting through old Czech documents with Marie and looking at the images of the terribly young men who gave their lives that others might be free, I have not changed my relationship with my father. But by shedding light on what happened to each of these individuals who touched our families, we have gained an understanding that is balm to old wounds. In learning about the crew, its last mission and its fate, we have joined those whose mission is to remember. John captured this idea when he directed me to a quote from the poet William Wordsworth: "We will grieve not, rather find strength in what remains behind…"

If we encounter these old ghosts in our lives going forward, we won't fear them. We will thank them for their sacrifice; acknowledge their pain; and assure them that they live on in places where past and present coexist—on Dubec Hill, in Pradlo, in Nepomuk, and within us.

MEMORIAL DAY 2015: JOHN TORRISON, SKIPPER GODDARD MILLER, BILL BOYCE,
AND GEORGE TORRISON VISIT THE CREW'S COMMON GRAVE AT JEFFERSON BARRACKS NATIONAL CEMETERY.

EPILOGUE

On Memorial Day 2015, we stood—Skipper Miller, John and George Torrison, and I—gazing on the shared grave of ten men who, without having the chance to know it, had exerted such a profound influence on our lives. We came to the Jefferson Barracks National Cemetery near St. Louis from our homes and families in different sections of America, called together by a mission—just as these ten men had been, all those decades earlier. We came, in honor of the holiday, to pay our respects and give our thanks to George, Kandy, Dusty, Joe, Charles, Oscar, Wayne, Harold, Roy and John. Skipper wore George Goddard's Ennis High School class ring on a chain around her neck.

I thought about Leona Kandarian's November 1943 letter to Haig, in which she expressed a hope that Haig, Joe Altemus and Charles Spickard "won't ever have to be separated from each other." In fact, they will not. The members of Miss Fortune's crew are still together on their last mission, and they always will be.

The program for the day's events reported that the 564 group burial sites at Jefferson Barracks represent the largest total of such sites in any VA national cemetery. I was struck by the cemetery's more personal connection to the crew. It is fitting that their common grave is located near where Rexford Rhodes enlisted in 1941 and Haig Kandarian received a portion of his training later that year. Of the Miss Fortune crew members at rest there, Missouri native Rhodes and southern Illinoisan Harold Carter may have come closest to being buried at home.

Standing in the warm sunlight on a lush green lawn next to a bright white marker, I puzzled over the feeling that overtook me as we chatted and snapped pictures. There was sadness, to be sure, but less than I had expected. The scene felt less like graveside mourning and more like...a family reunion. It was in a sense—a family of families brought together by Miss Fortune. We talked about the crew, our children and grandchildren, family history, pictures and the things going on in our lives. Perhaps we unconsciously had fallen back into the old crew family habit of exchanging information in round-robin fashion, but without need of letters, postage and Grace Altemus Hodgson's typing skills.

The moment was doubly bittersweet. Barely a month earlier, we had learned from Cocoa Beach that Grace had died at age ninety-five. Grace. Whose letter sharing Ray Noury's narrative had done so much, then and still, to bind our families together. Grace was gone from us now, lost to us like so many others. Her obituary reported that her ashes will be interred with those of her husband, Col. Reginald M. "Bud" Hodgson, Jr., at Arlington National Cemetery. That, too, is fitting.

As we headed back to our cars from the gravesite, I thought about Ray's remarks in Nepomuk when he expressed admiration for the Czechs' overwhelming show of gratitude to him, to Miss Fortune's crew—and, by extension, to all Americans who fought to defeat the Nazis. I had seen that gratitude on display myself in 2014. My visit to the crew's grave hardly registered as thanks for their sacrifice. But it's a start.

Time and again during the research for this book, I was stopped cold by the thought of ten futures extinguished in one moment. It was an abstract thought at first. But it became real and immediate as I encountered the tangible evidence of those unrealized futures.

A sentence in a long-dead co-pilot's letter to his sister. A catch in the voice as a widow's sacrifice was relived. Wedding portraits and crew photographs featuring smiling young men whose air of confidence—whether genuine or merely feigned for the camera—underscores the dread for those who look at the pictures today knowing Regensburg was on the horizon.

At some level I understood this crew was tough. As I learned more, I got an inkling of just how tough the crew members really were. They knew the odds for their long missions to Germany were terrible. They knew they were in for it. But they suppressed their fear, climbed in their B-24, did the job and willingly paid the price.

I saw the same toughness when I first looked at Evelyn Goddard's expression at the medal ceremony. I saw it while Ray, Grace and Wanda sat in sun-splashed rooms seventy years and many miles distant from Dubec Hill, speaking softly in their old age about hard memories. This was not a façade of detachment created by walling off the painful things or keeping them at arm's length. It was, instead, the sad resilience earned by living every day of every year for many years with profound loss.

I recognized the look. I'd seen it on my father's face. Perhaps, if he had lived longer, he would have reached the point at which he was ready to tell the story.

That the crew's story came to be told at all is remarkable. This is due to the dedicated citizens of the Czech Republic, who kept the story alive in secret for forty years and then used their newly won freedom to tell the world. It is due to John Torrison, who has tirelessly called, written, emailed, researched, copied, scanned and traveled in search of the crew's history and families for more than a decade. He found Ray, Skipper, Grace, Wanda—and so many others. And it is due to the skill and insight of John DeMers, who turned an overhelming mass of facts into an understandable narrative by writing with a reporter's eye and son's heart. They made a mission out of Miss Fortune's last mission.

And what of my mission launched with an impulsive call to Ray Noury in 2013? This book began as an effort to learn more about one man. I wanted to know the things my father would not dis-cuss—and, perhaps, to understand better why he toggled so easily between warmth and distance, affection and anger. I wanted to know why life in our home was equal parts *Leave it to Beaver* and *Saving Private Ryan*. I wanted to learn what my mother knew as she loved, nursed and occasionally battled with "My Bill" during forty-plus years of marriage.

The December 19, 1943 mission to Augsburg initially captured my attention. That was, after all, the crucial mission when "some-thing bad" happened to William D. Boyce—the defining moment that saved his life by nearly killing him. Decades after the fact, defining any one moment that defined him is a challenge.

Comparing Ray's oral history to details in letters reminded me of the lesson that any courtroom lawyer will teach about what hap-pens at trial: Eyewitnesses describe the same event differently.

Ray recollected that my father's wound resulted from a flak burst. In her April 1944 letter recounting a hospital visit with my father, Grace Altemus Hodgson reported a different version. My fa-ther told Grace that an attacking German fighter was firing 20 mm cannon shells at the B-24's side when a shell entered the plane and detonated next to my father's right leg. That version fits with an interview my father gave to a Cleveland newspaper while he was hospitalized. "The flier...said the shot hit his leg sideways. He re-marked: 'Lucky it wasn't a direct slap or I wouldn't have anything of this leg to show.'" That version also meshes with a reference in another letter written by Mel Adams, who flew as the engineer on the December 19 mission to Augsburg. Adams wrote of my father: "He sure was a valuable fellow to lose. Guess you know he got his Jerry after he was hit. He was put in for the D.F.C. but don't know whether he received it. George put him in for it."

Flak burst or cannon shell, two facts become clear when mul-tiple eyewitness accounts are matched up with the Sortie Report for December 19, 1943. One is that my father was hit in the leg and then kept firing his .50 caliber waist gun until he shot down the attacking ME 110. The other is that, despite his own shrapnel wounds, Ray saved my father's life. That's enough certainty for me. And reason enough to have traveled to Ray's Rhode Island home in

July 2013 to thank him in person seventy years after the fact.

I nearly waited too long. Ray died on December 20, 2013—exactly seventy years and one day after the mission to Augsburg.

Knowing one man required me to know eleven others. They flew with and in place of my father as 1943 became 1944. They remained with him for the next four decades, and although I did not recognize it at the time, they shadowed my childhood.

BILL AND PEGGY BOYCE IN 1983.

Though my father wouldn't talk about the war in his later years, I think about the brief time when he was willing to describe his thoughts. I think about the May 1944 letter to Roy Hughes's mother that Wanda so graciously gave to me. He signed it "Billy." He told her that "it is good...to be able to write to you, + all the parents of the fellows." He continued: "As you say, I was so close too. It is as if we were coming home one at a time, + I happened to be the first—+ [I] am just writing to fill in while the others return."

When we shared the same home, I mistook my father's long silences for apathy. I thought he was the least sentimental guy around. But there was nothing apathetic about the wounded vet who wrote his missing buddy's mother and told her, "Goodbye for now Mom—look on that Mother's Day's card—it's from Roy—by me." Like Mel Adams and many others, he simply kept his sentiment and his thoughts to himself after coming home. It's tempting to speculate that his choice not to talk caused the steam and eruptions I feared as a child. I have decided to skip the speculation because, as it turns out, I don't really need an explanation. Knowing the story is enough. And knowing it, I'm not surprised that he struggled at times after the war. I'm surprised he was able to live his life as well as he did.

Once I better understood what happened during his last flight, I wanted to know what my father thought about his kill-or-be-killed encounter with an attacking Luftwaffe fighter. I read and reread the letter from Grace recounting my father's hospital-bed description of his crew in combat. My father told Grace that "he saw those boys when they were in actual combat—when they were surrounded by the enemy—and he told me how cool they were." He also told her: "It wasn't that they weren't scared or that they were brave. But they all had so much to them—and they were so well trained—that they did what was expected of them and more." Dad answered my question years before I asked it.

I long have wondered why he didn't talk about the war. As the first one home he may have thought that any remotely boastful-sounding descriptions would violate his sense of a survivor's obligations. Practical man that he was, he probably saw no point to a wrenching conversation that would resurrect his worst memories without changing what had happened to him and his buddies. Perhaps, too, he thought his son didn't really need to know just how awful "something bad" could be.

What would my father have done if I had worked up the nerve and asked him to talk? He might have refused. He probably would have gotten mad. Or gone silent. Even if he had opened up, I realize now that I could not have absorbed the story while he was alive.

As Roy Hughes recognized when he dreamed of irrigating the desert soil, preparation precedes growth. For me to obtain a fuller grasp of this crew's sacrifice, of what they gave up and what their families took on, I had to live some life first—love and marriage, birth and death, hope and relief, elation, pain, grief, uncertainty, fear and worry.

My father could not have told me the things he knew. What he knew, and what I wanted to know, must be felt.

Now, I know.

ABOUT THE AUTHORS

WILLIAM J. BOYCE lives in Houston, Texas, where he practiced law for eighteen years before becoming a justice on the state court of appeals. He graduated from Northwestern University's Medill School of Journalism, and from Northwestern University School of Law. Before attending law school, he worked for newspapers in Illinois and Oregon. He is married to Maria Wyckoff Boyce and is the proud father of daughters Emily and Julia.

JOHN HARTLEY TORRISON studied art and religion at Wagner College, the New School, and the California College of Arts and Crafts. He has worked as a studio potter, art teacher, sailmaker for Pete Seeger's *Clearwater* and for thirty years as a cabinetmaker. John lives with his wife Christine in Westbrook, CT near all of their grandchildren: Hartley, Skye, Sven, Isabella and Shiloh. His interest in genealogy and American history began a thirteen-year journey to discover the lost details of his uncle's WWII military service. That search brought clarity and honor to his family and to all the crew's families.

JOHN DeMERS is a veteran author and news reporter, having earned bylines in 136 foreign countries. He has worked for newspapers in Baton Rouge, LA, Jackson, MS and Houston, TX, in addition to spending many years as a writer and editor for United Press International in his native New Orleans and on the Foreign Desk in Washington, D.C.